Lecture Notes in Business Information Processing   452

More information about this series at https://link.springer.com/bookseries/7911

Jochen De Weerdt · Artem Polyvyanyy (Eds.)

Intelligent Information Systems

CAiSE Forum 2022
Leuven, Belgium, June 6–10, 2022
Proceedings

 Springer

Editors
Jochen De Weerdt (iD)
KU Leuven Research Center for Information
Systems Engineering (LIRIS)
Leuven, Belgium

Artem Polyvyanyy (iD)
The University of Melbourne
Carlton, VIC, Australia

ISSN 1865-1348   ISSN 1865-1356 (electronic)
Lecture Notes in Business Information Processing
ISBN 978-3-031-07480-6   ISBN 978-3-031-07481-3 (eBook)
https://doi.org/10.1007/978-3-031-07481-3

This Springer imprint is published by the registered company Springer Nature Switzerland AG
The registered company address is: Gewerbestrasse 11, 6330 Cham, Switzerland

Preface

The CAiSE conference series provides a platform for exchanging experiences, preliminary research results, and ideas between academia and industry in the field of information systems engineering. The conference serves as the annual worldwide meeting point for the community of information system engineers. The 34th edition of the CAiSE conference was organized by the Faculty of Economics and Business (KU Leuven) and the Faculty of Economics and Business Administration (Ghent University) and conducted in Leuven, Belgium, during June 6–10, 2022. This edition of the conference put a special emphasis on the theme of information systems in the post-COVID era.

The CAiSE Forum is a place at the CAiSE conference for presenting and discussing new ideas and tools related to information systems engineering. Intended to serve as an interactive platform, the Forum aims to present emerging topics and controversial positions and demonstrate innovative systems, tools, and applications. The Forum sessions facilitate the interaction, discussion, and exchange of ideas among presenters and participants. Similar to other recent Forum editions, two types of submissions were invited in 2022:

- Visionary papers that present innovative research projects and are still at a relatively early stage and do not necessarily include a full-scale validation.
- Demo papers that describe innovative tools and prototypes which implement the results of research efforts.

Each submission to the Forum was reviewed by three Program Committee (PC) members. Submissions that achieved a consensus on relevance, novelty, and rigour were accepted for presentation at the Forum. Some papers were invited to the Forum as a result of the evaluation process in the CAiSE main research track. Each such invited paper was reviewed by two PC members. Altogether, 15 papers were accepted for presentation at the Forum out of the total of 24 full paper submissions. The accepted papers are collected in this volume. These papers were presented at dedicated sessions of the CAiSE conference.

We want to thank all the contributors to the CAiSE 2022 Forum. Firstly, we thank the PC members for their timely and high-quality reviews and help promoting the event. Secondly, we thank the Program Chairs of the CAiSE conference, Geert Poels and Xavier Franch, for their assistance with handling the papers invited from the main research track. Thirdly, we thank all the authors of the papers for sharing their work with the community. Finally, we thank Monique Snoeck and Frederik Gailly, the General Chairs of the CAiSE 2022 conference, and the conference's Local Organizing Committee for their support in coordinating the paper presentations at the conference and their publication.

June 2022

Jochen De Weerdt
Artem Polyvyanyy

Organization

Forum Chairs

Jochen De Weerdt   Katholieke Universiteit Leuven, Belgium
Artem Polyvyanyy   University of Melbourne, Australia

Program Committee

João Paulo Almeida	Federal University of Espírito Santo, Brazil
Abel Armas Cervantes	University of Melbourne, Australia
Adriano Augusto	University of Melbourne, Australia
Jörg Becker	University of Münster, Germany
Devis Bianchini	University of Brescia, Italy
Andrea Burattin	Technical University of Denmark, Denmark
Corentin Burnay	University of Namur, Belgium
Cristina Cabanillas	University of Seville, Spain
Diego Calvanese	Free University of Bozen-Bolzano, Italy
Cinzia Cappiello	Politecnico di Milano, Italy
Carlo Combi	Università degli Studi di Verona, Italy
Maxime Cordy	University of Luxembourg, Luxembourg
Maya Daneva	University of Twente, The Netherlands
Johannes De Smedt	Katholieke Universiteit Leuven, Belgium
Chiara Di Francescomarino	Fondazione Bruno Kessler-IRST, Italy
Cristina Gómez	Universitat Politècnica de Catalunya, Spain
Faruk Hasić	KU Leuven, Belgium
Jan Jürjens	University of Koblenz-Landau, Germany
Marite Kirikova	Riga Technical University, Latvia
Agnes Koschmider	Kiel University, Germany
Sander J. J. Leemans	RWTH Aachen, Germany
Henrik Leopold	Kühne Logistics University, Germany
Andrea Marrella	Sapienza University of Rome, Italy
Massimo Mecella	Sapienza University of Rome, Italy
Michele Melchiori	University of Brescia, Italy
Marco Montali	Free University of Bozen-Bolzano, Italy
Pierluigi Plebani	Politecnico di Milano, Italy
Manuel Resinas	University of Seville, Spain
Wenjie Ruan	University of Exeter, UK
Anthony Simonofski	University of Namur, Belgium

Tijs Slaats   University of Copenhagen, Denmark
Kari Smolander   Lappeenranta University of Technology, Finland
Arnon Sturm   Ben-Gurion University, Israel
Angelo Susi   Fondazione Bruno Kessler-IRST, Italy
Han van der Aa   University of Mannheim, Germany
Dirk van der Linden   University of Northumbria, UK
Boudewijn van Dongen   Eindhoven University of Technology,
                                     The Netherlands
Irene Vanderfeesten   Open University of the Netherlands,
                                     The Netherlands
Jan Vanthienen   KU Leuven, Belgium
Panos Vassiliadis   University of Ioannina, Greece
Ingo Weber   Technical University of Berlin, Germany

Contents

An Architecture for Food Product Recommendation Focusing on Nutrients and Price

Rian das Dores Alves[1(✉)], José Maria David[1], Regina Braga[1],
Kennya Siqueira[2], Guilherme Barbosa[1], João P. Costa[1], Victor Ströele[1],
and Eduardo Barrére[1]

[1] Departament of Computer Science, Federal University of Juiz de Fora, Juiz de
Fora, MG, Brazil
{rian.alves,guilhermebarbosa,joao.costa,
victor.stroele,eduardo.barrere}@ice.ufjf.br,
{jose.david,regina.braga}@ufjf.edu.br
[2] Embrapa Gado de Leite, Juiz de Fora, MG, Brazil
{kennya.siqueira}@embrapa.br

Abstract. Part of the world's population is nutrient deficient, a phenomenon known as hidden hunger. Poor eating conditions cause this deficiency, leading to illnesses and recovery difficulties. Malnourished patients are more easily affected by Covid-19 and have a difficult recovery after the illness. An effective food choice has the price and nutritional value of food products as the most relevant factors, with the price being the most relevant, considering the context of countries such as Brazil. Thus, having identified a scenario in which the access and food price mainly cause malnutrition. This work proposes an architecture, called Nutri'n Price, to recommend high nutritional foods with low costs. The architecture encompasses a network of ontologies, inference algorithms, information retrieval and collaborative filtering techniques to recommend the best foods according to nutrient choice, price, and user contextual information. A prototype of a mobile application was developed to evaluate the feasibility of the proposed architecture.

Keywords: Food · Recommendation · Ontology network · Information retrieval · Collaborative filtering

1 Introduction

The world society lives with the double burden of malnutrition so that about $1/3$ of humanity is nutrient deficient [4]. This phenomenon, called Hidden Hunger, is mainly generated by poor feeding conditions, causing the onset of diseases, reducing productivity levels, and decreasing the population's life expectancy [9]. The global pandemic caused by the SARS-CoV-2 virus highlights how malnutrition can influence getting or recovering from illness[2].

Different reasons can cause nutrient deficiencies, such as food prices, lack of nutritional knowledge, availability of products, among others. However, food

© The Author(s), under exclusive license to Springer Nature Switzerland AG 2022
J. De Weerdt and A. Polyvyanyy (Eds.): CAiSE Forum 2022, LNBIP 452, pp. 1–9, 2022.
https://doi.org/10.1007/978-3-031-07481-3_1

choice has as one of the most relevant factors the price of food products, being more relevant than the nutritional value, directly affecting the quality of the population's diet [9]. The increase in the cost of staple foods, accentuated by the COVID-19 pandemic, may cause even more restrictions on the purchase of products, especially for populations with lower income [1,9].

In this context, Embrapa[1] (Brazilian Agricultural Research Corporation), in partnership with the Federal University of Juiz de Fora, developed the Nutrileite Project [9,10]. The objective of the project is to develop computer systems that help in choosing food products based on their nutritional cost-benefit ratio. As far as we are concerned, there is no complete, safe, and free source of data to calculate the cost of nutrients and help the consumer purchase cheaper products with nutritional quality.

This work aims to propose an architecture, called Nutri'n Price, that provides, in an intelligent and personalized way, information related to food products, considering the essential nutrients and the costs associated with these foods and nutrients. The architecture encompasses an ontology network as a knowledge base to support recommendation techniques based on information retrieval, collaborative filtering, intelligent processing and knowledge discovery. Nutri'n Price is made available to consumers through a mobile application that uses price data extracted from supermarket websites. These data, together with data from users and nutritional values of foods, feeds the knowledge base that, based on inference algorithms, recommends products with high nutritional value, low cost and easy access to the consumer.

The ontology network also includes definitions and information about the user's profile, food products and nutrients. This network uses metadata and information from multiple sources to process the recommendation [3,8]. We have not identified any approach in the literature that uses an ontology network that covers different contexts and uses intelligent techniques for recommending products considering the relationship between nutritional value and cost. In this sense, our approach is innovative, using a semantic knowledge base and intelligent techniques to recommend nutritionally adequate products at a low cost, adapted to the consumer's profile. In [7], the approach focuses on the nutritional composition of foods and how this information could support health sectors. Nutri'n Price focuses on analyzing the cost of nutrients and user's preferences to recommend the cheapest and healthiest foods. Gunawardena et al. [6] address, like Nutri'n Price, the recommendation of foods to the consumer. However, the recommendation is made in the context of restaurants and not in foods to be consumed in everyday life. Furthermore, we use different recommendation techniques. Nutri'n Price uses a knowledge base and intelligent techniques (reasoner) to recommend products and rate similar users.

This article is organized into the following sections, in addition to the Introduction. Section 2 describes the proposed architecture and recommendation steps. Section 3 presents usage scenario. Finally, in Sect. 4, conclusions are drawn and possibilities for future work are listed.

---

[1] Embrapa Gado de Leite, https://www.embrapa.br.

2 Nutri'n Price Architecture

For the recommendation to be executed, we must have the users' profiles with their dietary restrictions, diseases, and preferences. We will use these profiles to define recommendations in future search requests. Our recommendation strategy is based on direct information retrieval in an ontology network and on collaborative filtering performed after processing inference algorithms on the network. A similarity algorithm uses the Jaccard Index [5], to define more similar users and recommend food products in the collaborative filtering context. The ontology network comprises the Food Ontology and User Ontology ontologies, developed by these authors, and the Human Disease Ontology[2], developed by health organizations and researchers at the University of Maryland. The database with the foods and nutrients was previously built by Embrapa. Food price data are taken from supermarkets. After extraction, the cost-effectiveness of nutrients and nutritional density are calculated. The methodology adopted to calculate costs and nutritional density were also previously applied by researchers at Embrapa [9,10]. After the calculations, the products are ranked and displayed. Figure 1 presents an overview of the architecture Nutri'n Price developed.

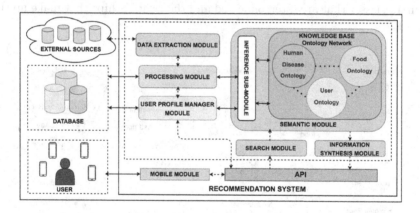

Fig. 1. Overview of the architecture nutri'n price.

The **Data Extraction Module** defines the periods and captures data related to the prices of food products. The aim is to keep prices always up to date, to offer an updated recommendation to the user. After, the data are sent to the **Processing Module**, this module calculates the cost of nutrients and the nutritional density of each food and stores the information.

The **User Profile Manager Module** manages user profiles. The **Search Module** is responsible for connecting and sending requests (nutrients, food, among others) to the **Semantic Module** (detailed in Sect. 2.1). The latter is responsible for selecting the recommended products, based on choosing one or

---

[2] Human Disease Ontology, https://disease-ontology.org/.

more nutrients of interest (sent via the **Search Module**). The **Inference sub-module** accesses the knowledge base formed by the ontology network, logic rules and inference machine to carry out the recommendations. After semantic processing, the information is sent to the **Information Synthesis Module**, which organizes the information and makes it available for consumption by the API. The **Mobile Module** allows users to interact with the recommendation architecture through the API.

2.1   Semantic Module

The Ontology Network is used as a semantic model to support recommendations. Its main objective is to process the information (instances) from a set of logical rules and inference algorithms and from new relationships and classifications, to recommend foods suitable for a given nutritional need of the population or specific user, considering the cost of food. The Ontology Network is dynamic, as instances representing different contexts are processed and information is inferred for the recommendation of the most accessible food products. This network is formed by classes and relationships encompassing the Food Ontology, User Ontology and the Human Disease Ontology. Figure 2 illustrates some of the main classes that are interconnected and the relationships that make up the network.

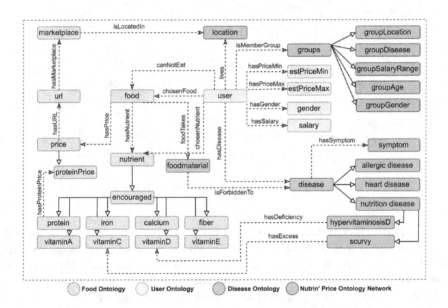

Fig. 2. Ontology network

Food Ontology defines the concepts related to food products (:food), nutrients (:nutrient), specific nutrients (e.g. :protein and :vitaminA), price of each product for each 100g (:price), price of each nutrient (e.g. :proteinPrice and :vitaminAPrice), URL of the websites where the product was searched (:url), the supermarket where the product was found (:marketplace) and the location where this supermarket is found (:location). In addition to classes, the network specifies relationships, through object properties, such as the relationship between the :food class and the :nutrient subclasses, which indicate the amounts of nutrients present for each food. The Food Ontology also has the relationships between food, price, url and supermarket, to identify in which web address the prices were searched (:hasURL), in which establishment (:hasMarketplace), and from which location (:isLocatedIn). User Ontology was created to represent concepts related to users. There is the class that represents the user (:User), user location (:location), food restrictions (:foodRestriction) and diseases (:disease). In addition to the classes, the object properties relate these concepts to the user.

Disease Ontology privileges the definition of concepts that refer to diseases that are related to nutrition and food are highlighted here. We can see the classes directly related to nutritional diseases (:nutrition disease) and nutrient deficiency (:nutritional deficiency disease).We also highlight food allergies that exist and are represented by classes such as :food allergy and its sub classes. Some classes relate these allergies to the materials that cause them (:foodmaterial). We can also highlight the class that defines the symptoms of each disease (:symptom). There are few object properties used in this set of disease ontology classes. The use of Disease Ontology classes is crucial for the recommendation of food products, as it supports the discovery of nutrients and restricted foods according to the user's illness.

The ontology network considers that smaller ontologies are more extensible and easier to maintain and reuse, with clear concepts and relationships. Moreover, the connection between these ontologies enhances semantics and enables the discovery of new knowledge related to the recommendation. The network is attributed to creating new classes, object properties, properties chains and rules to assist the processing and provide new knowledge to the application. Classes semantically equivalent have been merged into just one, as is the case with :location. We created new classes to define groups according to user characteristics, these are represented by the :groups class and its sub classes. In addition, to connect the ontologies and semantically enrich the network, we created object properties, in which :chosenNutrient (defines the nutrients chosen by the user), :chosenFood (defines the foods chosen by the user) and the : hasDisease (defines the diseases the user can have). We also highlight the creation of property chains, such as :canNotEat, which through various relationships can infer, through reasoner, that a user should not consume foods against his dietary restrictions.

All classes, relationships and rules developed or reused in the network aimed to build a structure that supported information retrieval techniques or collaborative filtering for the recommendation. Property chains, such as: canNotEat, assist in the direct retrieval of information and returning food that we should not consume. We also developed SWRL rules to support in processing new ontological relationships. These SWRL rules define groups that identify users with similar preferences or characteristics. One of the advantages of this approach is that recommendation systems based on ontology, mitigate cold start problems due to the possibility of retrieving information related to a particular user with the help of a reasoner and inference rules.

2.2   Recommendation Steps

The recommendation approach used by Nutri'n Price is hybrid, it consists of the combined use of information retrieval and collaborative filtering techniques, supported by the ontology network. We chose the hybrid approach to provide a more accurate recommendation. We detail the recommendation steps from the process flow illustrated in Fig. 3. The recommendation process starts with checking restricted foods for a user or user groups and choosing the target nutrient. Then, the Nutri'n Price checks the mandatory restrictions by retrieving information in the ontology network, considering the foods that the user cannot consume. For the execution of these restrictions, the reasoning is executed in the network and all inferences of the relation :canNotEat (:user - :canNotEat - : food) for one or more individuals must be stored in a list with restricted foods.

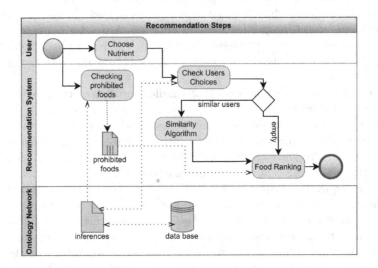

Fig. 3. Process flow for recommendation

Associated with the verification of restrictions, one or more target nutrients must also be sent to Nutri'n Price, making it possible to recommend foods rich in the selected nutrient(s). Next, Nutri'n Price should check for similar users, that are, users who previously chose the same nutrients. For this, the ontology network is queried through the object property :nutrientChoosen, the inverse of :chosenNutrient (:user :chooseNutrient :nutrient), so that all similar users are returned. Then, the ontological network is processed to define groups according to the comparison between the requesting user(s) and similar users. A set with groups subsets of each similar user is defined. The groups of each similar user are compared with the groups of requesting users through the approach called Jaccard similarity, to support the precision and accuracy of the recommendations. Figure 4 exemplifies how the Jaccard index is used.

In Fig. 4, the comparison is performed using subsets of groups relevant to a requesting user, named "Carlos" and two previous users, "Marcos" and "Maria". In Fig. 4 , we chose sets with few groups to facilitate understanding. As can be seen in Fig. 4, "Maria" is more similar to "Carlos" than "Marcos", since the similarity index of "Maria" is higher than that of "Marcos", with JIMaria = 0.6, while JIMarcos = 0.286. Therefore, in the ranking, the food product chosen by "Maria" for that nutrient is more suitable for "Carlos" than the product chosen by "Marcos" for that nutrient.

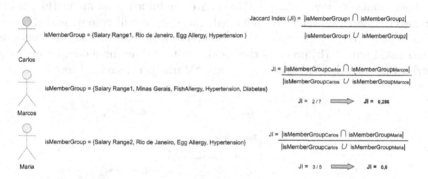

Fig. 4. Jaccard similarity between the requesting user "Carlos" and two previous users, "Marcos" and "Maria".

For the creation of the ranking, the restricted foods for the user, the similarity between the requesting user(s) and previous users, the nutritional density, the cost-effectiveness of the nutrient and the food prices are considered. The products are presented ordered according to the choice of nutrient and similarity between users. While similar, some products are restricted for the requesting user and not restricted for previous users, so we will compare the returned foods to those on the requesting user's banned foods list. If there are restricted foods, these must be removed from the products to be recommended.

3   Usage Scenario

This scenario considers a support group for poor people and with a previous history of COVID-19 is accompanied by the City Hall of Três Rios, Rio de Janeiro, Brazil. One of the nutritionists, named "Maria", knows the reality of each of her patients. She knows which of them are employed, their salary range, whether they receive government benefits, what illnesses they have and their dietary restrictions. To assist in the construction of diets and food choices for these patients, given their social and financial vulnerability, in addition to symptoms of previous illnesses and sequels left by COVID-19, the nutritionist uses Nutri'n Price to recommend the food. Nutri'n Price helps in decision making to verify which products must be purchased to be distributed.

The nutritionist "Maria" has an appointment with the patient "José", which complains of excessive sleep, weak body and constant infections. The nutritionist suspects that "José" has low immunity, as he works as a merchant in crowded environments, running significant risks of contracting COVID-19 and spreading the disease. Thus, "Maria" recommends a diet rich in Vitamins A, C and E, nutrients that help immunity. "José" is 56 years old, has fish allergy, high blood pressure and diabetes. He should avoid foods rich in salt and sugar, and don't eat fish foods. All three nutrients have already undergone previous consultations, so the recommendations will be based on former users who chose these nutrients and have similarities with "José". Thus, once the information about the patient is registered and the nutrients indicated, the system will recommend the best products. Figure 5 (a) illustrates the mobile interface with the choice of vitamin C nutrient. Figure 5 (b) presents the ranking with the recommendation made by Nutri'n Price to "José". Figure 5(c) shows "Maria"'s choice for "José".

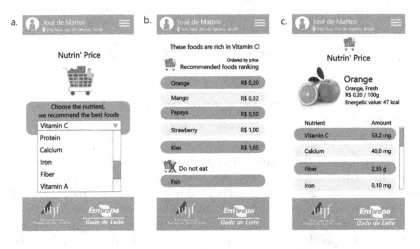

Fig. 5. Nutrin' price results for user "José" and details of the chosen food.

For the recommendation, previous users who chose these nutrients were checked. Vitamin C was chosen by more than 100 people, making it possible to calculate the similarity between them and "José". The 10 most similar were automatically chosen to compose the ranking, and displayed their food choices for Vitamin C. In addition, "Maria" also ordered the ranking by price and indicated to "José" the cheapest and good nutritional density. With that, the nutritionist can recommend foods that can increase the patient's immunity and thus be more resistant to COVID-19.

4 Conclusions

This work proposed an architecture, called Nutri'n Price, whose core is formed by the Semantic Module. The proposed solution aims to support consumers and nutrition professionals in decision-making for purchasing food products. We used an ontology net-work that considers, in addition to food, prices, and nutritional value, possible diseases caused by nutritional deficiencies. COVID-19 and its impacts on the lives of convalescent people stand out.

As future work, we propose the extension of the ontology network, to provide multidisciplinary views that add value to the recommendation. Furthermore, a formal and comprehensive experiment must be conducted to evaluate the Nutri'n Price solution effectively.

References

1. Baccarin, J.G., de Oliveira, J.A.: Inflação de alimentos no brasil em período da pandemia da covid 19, continuidade e mudanças. Segurança Alimentar e Nutricional **28**, e021002–e021002 (2021)
2. Diniz, D.M., Costa, Y.D.S., da Silva, A.M., de Andrade Aoyama, E.: Comprometimento do estado nutricional em pacientes com covid-19. Revista Brasileira Interdisciplinar de Saúde (2021)
3. Elali, R.: An intention mining approach using ontology for contextual recommendations. In: Krogstie, J., Ouyang, C., Ralyté, J. (eds.) Proceedings of the Doctoral Consortium Papers Presented at the 33rd International Conference on Advanced Information Systems Engineering (CAiSE 2021), Melbourne, Australia, June 28 - July 2, 2021. CEUR Workshop Proceedings, vol. 2906, pp. 69–78. CEUR-WS.org (2021)
4. Emadi, M.H., Rahmanian, M.: Commentary on challenges to taking a food systems approach within the food and agriculture organization (FAO). In: Squires, V.R., Gaur, M.K. (eds.) Food Security and Land Use Change under Conditions of Climatic Variability, pp. 19–31. Springer, Cham (2020). https://doi.org/10.1007/978-3-030-36762-6_2
5. Esteban, A., Zafra, A., Romero, C.: Helping university students to choose elective courses by using a hybrid multi-criteria recommendation system with genetic optimization. Knowl.-Based Syst. **194**, 105385 (2020)
6. Gunawardena, D., Sarathchandra, K.: Bestdish: A digital menu and food item recommendation system for restaurants in the hotel sector. In: 2020 International Conference on Image Processing and Robotics (ICIP), pp. 1–7. IEEE (2020)
7. Harrington, R.A., Adhikari, V., Rayner, M., Scarborough, P.: Nutrient composition databases in the age of big data: foodDB, a comprehensive, real-time database infrastructure. BMJ open **9**(6), e026652 (2019)
8. Padhiar, I., Seneviratne, O., Chari, S., Gruen, D., McGuinness, D.L.: Semantic modeling for food recommendation explanations. In: 2021 IEEE 37th International Conference on Data Engineering Workshops (ICDEW), pp. 13–19. IEEE (2021)
9. Siqueira, K.B., et al.: Custo benefício dos nutrientes dos alimentos consumidos no brasil. Ciência & Saúde Coletiva **25**, 1129–1135 (2020)
10. Siqueira, K.B., et al.: Nutrient density and affordability of foods in brazil by food group and degree of processing. Public Health Nutr. **24**(14), 4564–4571 (2021)

Advancing Data Architectures with Data Mesh Implementations

Inês Araújo Machado⏺, Carlos Costa⏺, and Maribel Yasmina Santos$^{(\boxtimes)}$ ⏺

ALGORITMI Research Center, University of Minho, Guimarães, Portugal
a80365@alunos.uminho.pt, {carlos.costa,maribel}@dsi.uminho.pt

Abstract. Data architectures have evolved over time to adapt to the growing needs of the business models. Recently, the Data Mesh concept emerged due to the limitations of current monolithic data architectures and the investments they require. It represents a paradigm shift in the way data architectures are thought and work, applying the microservices logic of software engineering to data engineering, and intends to make organizations truly data-driven, with data becoming the primary concern, leaving the data pipelines to secondary plan. These characteristics imply a change not only in the technological part of the data architecture, but also in the way the data teams are organized. Due to the youthfulness of the topic, it still lacks scientific foundation on the premises that are associated with it. Contributing to those foundations, this paper proposes a technological architecture for the implementation of a Data Mesh and evaluates the proposal with a demonstration case that highlights the usefulness and benefits of this type of data architecture.

Keywords: Data Mesh · Technological architecture · Data architectures

1 Introduction

Data Mesh represents a paradigm shift in data architectures. It consists of a decentralized data architecture that has as its main goal making data the primary concern of organizations [1]. Although the work of [1] takes the first steps in defining what might be the core concepts, principles and the logical architecture of a Data Mesh, these specifications are significantly high level, and there is still a lack of empiric, consolidated and validated scientific knowledge on the subject. Namely, this concept still lacks constructs, models (e.g., architectures), methods, and instantiations proposed through a research process ([8]). This paper aims to advance the state of the art in this field by proposing a technological architecture for the implementation of a Data Mesh and by evaluating this proposal with a demonstration case that highlights the usefulness and benefits of this type of data architecture, based on the premises previously formulated in the Data Mesh's domain model and conceptual architecture [7].

This paper is organized as follows. Section 2 introduces the related work. Section 3 presents the proposed technological architecture. Section 4 describes the demonstration

J. De Weerdt and A. Polyvyanyy (Eds.): CAiSE Forum 2022, LNBIP 452, pp. 10–18, 2022.
https://doi.org/10.1007/978-3-031-07481-3_2

case, highlighting how the several components of the conceptual architecture comple-
ment each other. Section 5 discusses the results and contribution of this work, for practitioners and organizations that move towards the effective and efficient implementation
of a Data Mesh, and concludes with some proposals for future work.

2   Related Work

According to [1], current monolithic architectures (such as Data Lakes [2] or Big Data
Warehouses [3]) do not meet the needs of the organizations, with the proper scalability
and democratization [4], and there is an inverse proportionality between the satisfaction
of their investors and the investment made in these architectures [5]. The proposal and
implementation of a Data Mesh needs to conform with four core concepts: domain-
oriented decentralized data ownership and architecture; data as a product; self-serve data
platform; and, federated computational governance [6]. The first concept is related to the
organization of the data and its ownership by the data teams themselves. The data teams
are organized considering the domains of the organization and the data responsibility is
decentralized by teams that integrate, besides engineers and data scientists, those who
work closely with the data [1]. The second concept, regarding seeing data as a product,
states that data must be the main concern of organizations, requiring high quality data [1]
that is one of the biggest difficulties when working with monolithic data architectures [6].
Analytical data is now seen as a product within organizations and, like any other product,
must meet quality standards and be available when needed. To be possible, data teams
(now called data product teams) need to have access to a high level infrastructure platform
[1]. This platform should provide the necessary set of services, so that each team can
use the technologies that best suits them to build, maintain and store their data products
[5]. All this diversity from node to node (in terms of teams, technologies, etc.) needs a
layer that harmonizes the Data Mesh, avoiding chaos and Data Silos. In this way, the last
core concept concerns a governance layer, with a federated computational governance
model that ensures interoperability within the Data Mesh. This model addresses the
complexity of the Data Mesh as a whole and establishes a set of rules to be followed
by all domains, ensuring that each domain maintains its independence to use the more
adequate technologies.

   Due to the youth of this concept, limited scientific and technical contributions are
available in the literature. Technical contributions were already addressed in [4, 5] and
[6]. Technological proposals are also scarce ([9] and [10]). To the best of our knowledge,
the first scientific contribution is related with our previous paper that proposes the Data
Mesh's domain model and conceptual architecture [7]. In this work, the domain model
fully describes a Data Mesh, including all its constructs and how they relate with each
other. The conceptual architecture is based on the premises that a Data Mesh is scalable
(e.g., can accommodate an infinite set of domains and datasets), user friendly (e.g., can
be easily implemented in any organization or context), and efficient (e.g., can provide fast
implementation of Mesh nodes and fast data consumption). Moreover, it complies with
the DATSIS (Discoverable, Addressable, Trustworthy, Self-describing, Interoperable
and Secure) principles for a Data Mesh. To make this concept tangible, and to guide
the implementation of a Data Mesh in real contexts, a technological architecture is now

proposed, translating the high-level knowledge of [1] into a technological architecture, as an artefact for the concretization of the Data Mesh Concept.

3   Technological Architecture for Data Mesh Implementations

The technological architecture defined and presented in this paper is based on a conceptual architecture resulting from the domain model established in [7] and the guiding principles summarized in the previous section (please refer to [7] to more details). Naturally, the conceptual architecture needs to be unfolded into a technological architecture (Fig. 1), aiming to present a wide range of technologies suitable to implement the components of the conceptual architecture [7]. Figure 1 and Fig. 2 correspond to the bridge established between the proposed conceptual architecture and the technologies that are feasible to implement it. Due to the broad scope of the conceptual architecture and the wide set of available technologies, the technological architecture has been divided into these two figures. The first presents the overall technological architecture of a Data Mesh as a whole, leaving the self-serve data platform component unspecified. Figure 2 presents in more detail all the technologies that are part of the self-serve data platform. It is intended that, with the presentation of the technological architecture, practitioners have available a starting point for the implementation of a Data Mesh. It should be noted that there are currently several other technologies on the market that can respond positively to the needs of the Data Mesh implementation, several of them listed in the figure, but many of them left out.

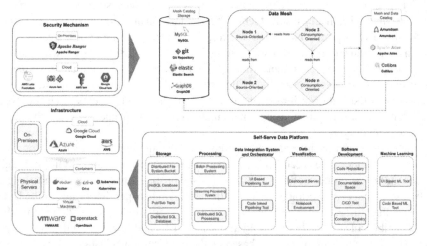

Fig. 1. Overall data mesh technological architecture

The choice of technologies integrated in these figures was based on two distinct criteria: 1) being open-source technologies (which implies a significant impact in reducing costs in the implementation of a Data Mesh) or 2) being services available in the Cloud (in AWS, Azure, and Google Cloud). In this sense, several Data Mesh implementations can

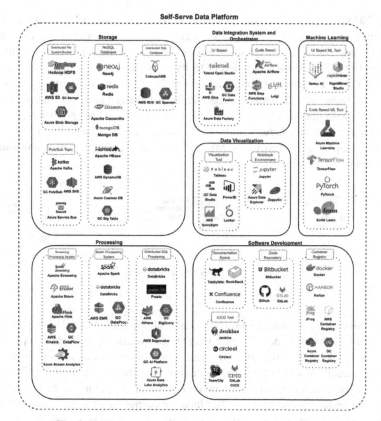

Fig. 2. Self-serve data platform technological architecture

be outlined, using combinations of these technologies. Each organization should reflect on the solutions presented and depending on the balance of their needs and resources, choose, amongst the various options, the one that will make more sense to use (in terms of cost, performance, and implementation difficulty).

4 Demonstration Case

This section presents a proof-of-concept of the proposed artifacts: domain model and conceptual architecture presented in [7], and the proposed technological architectures.

Scope and Node Organization. To illustrate a case that comes close to a real market need, the scope of the proof-of-concept will be a chocolate online seller company, with three domains of what is assumed to be the business itself. Thus, three domains will be created and published in the Data Mesh, namely: *Sales*, *Production*, and *Financial Management*. In the case of these three domains, it is considered that each one has one data product that originates one Mesh Node: *Online Sales*, *Product Cost*, and *Profits*. There are two source domains (*Sales* and *Production*) and one consumption domain

(*Financial Management*), since the join of the *Online Sales* data and *Product Cost* data will originate the calculation of the *Profits* generated in each sale. Note that, in this proof-of-concept, the aspect to emphasize is the flow of data throughout the architecture (Fig. 3) and not the complexity inherent to its transformations - since this can be as complex as the user wishes. Although the simplicity of the proof-of-concept, only three domains, the same: i) addresses the organization of the domains; ii) makes available data products with data quality concerns; iii) uses a high level infrastructure platform; iv) provides a governance layer with interoperability between the nodes. These are the four core principles described in the previous section. Many other domains and data products can now be added.

Fig. 3. Domains and data products

Infrastructure. In real contexts, the Data Mesh may be implemented in more than one cluster (in this proof-of-concept it is implemented within only one Hadoop cluster). In this cluster, a Docker container was created and, inside this container, an image of the Cloudera sandbox was instantiated, containing the Hadoop technology. To develop the data pipelines, each data product team makes use of Zeppelin Notebooks, using the language that better fits the team needs. Once the output data for each data product is ready, Apache Atlas (extended in this work for the Data Mesh requirements) is used to allow all the cataloging of the Data Mesh. In this case, the Apache Atlas repository serves as the Mesh Catalog Storage itself. For data visualization, besides being possible to use Zeppelin Notebooks, Power BI Desktop and Server were used to create and publish the visualizations. A script for automated analysis of data quality was created and indexed to each notebook, and its information transformed into a dashboard in Power BI. All the code created by each data product team must be documented and stored. Therefore, GitHub was used as a tool for storing and making code available. To have a direct communication channel in the Data Mesh, Slack was used, and direct channels were created between users and data teams/owners of the various data products. Regarding access (consumption list), a form was created, through Google Forms, where this access can be requested, and this information is forwarded to those entitled to it (e.g.: data product owners who can grant authorization access).

Folder Organization in HDFS. Revisiting the concept of domain, it is possible to understand domains as being the structured division of the organization by different business processes [1] (such as sales, customer service, logistics, etc.). However, depending on the size and complexity of the organization in question, domains may have more than one data product [7]. There must be a continuous concern to ensure that the various domains, and the teams that build and maintain these domains, can communicate with each other efficiently. For this reason, there is the need to ensure a governance approach that extends to the entire Data Mesh and respects the DATSIS principles. To keep the implementation aligned with the previous principles, a standard organization of the Data Mesh Nodes is proposed, which should be followed by all the teams, to implement these best practices in their domains and data products (Fig. 4).

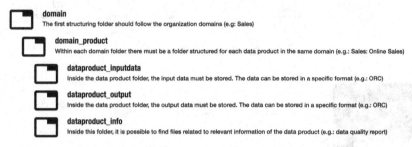

Fig. 4. Folder organization in HDFS

Databases and Tables Organization in Domains and Data Products. As for the HDFS folders that represent the various nodes of the Data Mesh, it is also necessary to think about how the domains and data products will be organized in the Hive Metastore. It was defined that a data product corresponds to a Hive database (collection of several tables). Also, domains are defined as being a collection of databases (of the various data products). Although the dataset of this proof-of-concept is not very complex, this will be the most proper way to organize the Hive Metastore, anticipating that the data products will evolve over time, given the dynamic nature of organizations.

Mesh and Data Catalog. One of the most important principles of Data Mesh is the complete discovery of the data that it holds by all its users. So, there is a component in the proof-of-concept where information about the data products is centralized, such as, for example, data lineage, data schema, and data quality information. Apache Atlas was chosen as the Mesh and Data Catalog. By default, Apache Atlas does not provide all this information to portray Hive tables and databases. Therefore, it was necessary to extend it. Figure 5 presents the proposed extension of the organization of the parameters *per* data product (Hive database) and the respective tables (Hive tables). A Data Product corresponds, in this proof-of-concept, to a Hive database. In turn, the various tables in a Data Product are the Hive tables, and the domains can be found by clustering the various databases (they can also be found by searching for their name in Apache Atlas).

Figure 6 shows the existing Data Products in the proposed Data Mesh. By selecting a given Data Product, and considering the Apache Atlas extension, it is possible to see the associated metadata: data product owner, dashboards access, and consumption list, among others. Inside a Data Product, it is possible to navigate and retrieve more details about the tables that are present in each data product's database. For each table, it is possible to access the data quality report and the code repository that fuels them. Figure 7 shows the extensions made to Apache Atlas to provide these features for each table.

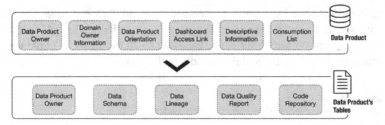

Fig. 5. Apache atlas type extensions

Fig. 6. List of existing data products in the data mesh

Properties	Lineage	Relationships	Classifications	Audits

Key	Value
aliases	product_cost
codeAccess	https://github.com/inesmachado98/Data-Mesh/tree/main/Production/Product_Cost
columns	id_product cost production_factory warehouse
comment	
dataProductOwner	DW_user1 https://app.slack.com/client/T02G59QQNUX/C02GL16JAJW
dataQuality	https://app.powerbi.com/groups/me/reports/471dedef-7cf0-4a97-888c-d34c0d438981/ReportSection4f278a296ca761a7e13
db	product_cost
description	Summarise the data regarding the distribution of each attribute through the corresponding factory and warehouse

Fig. 7. Data product table details

This is an example of the navigation flow that a Data Analyst can follow when discovering and investigating a new dataset. Thus, with the previously presented Apache Atlas extensions, it is possible to have a decentralized architecture with functional centralization when it comes to cataloging its various nodes and data. Figure 8 shows an example of an analytical data product dashboard "*Data Product: Product Cost Report*", analyzing the distribution of products among the various warehouses, the cost distributed by each one, and an analysis of the variation of production costs by the factories that produce them. As the presented dashboard is integrated in Apache Atlas, the Data Analyst can discover and comprehend the data that is involved in a report request. Furthermore, all the Data Products that exist in an organization will be available having all this metadata and information stored in one place – fulfilling all the DATSIS principles and the four core concepts of a Data Mesh.

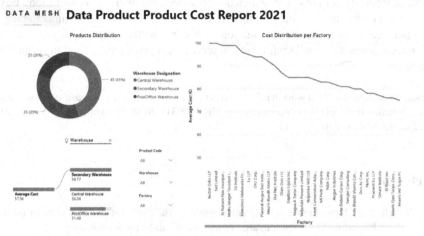

Fig. 8. Analytical dashboard of the product cost data product

Supporting Tools. To be able to provide all the information mentioned above in Apache Atlas, it was necessary to use additional tools.

5 Conclusion

This work focused on proposing and demonstrating a technological architecture (major gap identified in the literature) and discussing organizational aspects whenever applicable and relevant. This work allows an improved solidification on the technological part of Data Mesh which will support future implementers of this data architecture. It is important to be noted that the present implementation aims to also proof that a Data Mesh can be a simpler and familiar infrastructure, being adaptable to the various levels of complexity of the business models. Like any other architecture, it must be studied the need and use of this implementation before its building, being also possible to adapt the already existing structures (e.g.: an existing Data Warehouse can become a Mesh node). There are some key points that can still be pointed out as future work on this topic: the first and most related to the presented proof-of-concept, will be the full functional development of the consumption list, using technologies suitable for this purpose, such as the Apache Ranger. Next there are the challenges of mapping the data within the various data products so that, node to node, there is not too much replication of data and effort (the development of a framework that enables this mapping and helps contextualize the topic). There is also the challenge of "change": whether in terms of the impact that this paradigm shift has on the users in the organizations (in terms of reorganizing teams, for example), or in how the change of data within each data product will be handled in the Data Mesh as a whole. Finally, matters linked to the complexity of the architecture interoperability in complex contexts are also points of future work in what is the present evolution of data architectures. Data Mesh is progressing every day, as new contributions come in from all over the world, which does not mean that there is not still a long way to go when it comes to consolidating the subject. In summary, this paper aims to take the first practical steps in the implementation of this architecture, contributing with a proof of concept (even if in small scale) that can serve as a support for data architects and their teams.

Acknowledgements. This work has been supported by FCT – *Fundação para a Ciência e Tecnologia* within the R&D Units Project Scope: UIDB/00319/2020. This paper uses icons made by Freepik, from www.flaticon.com.

References

1. Dehghani, Z.: How to move beyond a monolithic data lake to a distributed data mesh, pp. 1–20 (2019). https://martinfowler.com/articles/data-monolith-to-mesh.html
2. Santos, M.Y., Costa, C.: Big Data Concepts, Warehousing, and Analytics. River Publishing, Denmark (2020)
3. Costa, C., Santos, M.Y.: Big data: state-of-the-art concepts, techniques, technologies, modeling approaches and research challenges. IAENG Int. J. Comput. Sci. **44**, 285–301 (2017)
4. Barr, M.: What is a Data Mesh — and How Not to Mesh it Up [Internet]. 2020 [cited 2020 Oct 29]. https://towardsdatascience.com/what-is-a-data-mesh-and-how-not-to-mesh-it-up-210710bb41e0
5. Dehghani, Z.: Data Mesh Paradigm Shift in Data Platform Architecture. San Francisco, USA: InfoQ; 2020. https://www.youtube.com/watch?v=52MCFe4v0UU
6. Dehghani Z. Data Mesh Principles and Logical Architecture [Internet]. 2020 [cited 2020 Dec 7]. Available from: https://martinfowler.com/articles/data-mesh-principles.html
7. Machado, I.A., Costa, C., Santos, M.Y.: Data-driven information systems: the data mesh paradigm shift. In: International Conference on Information Systems Development (ISD 2021)
8. Peffers, K., Tuunanen, T., Rothenberger, M.A., Chatterjee, S.: A design science research methodology for information systems research. J. Manag. Inf. Syst. **24**, 45–77 (2007)
9. Schultze, M., Wider, A.: Data mesh in practice: how Europe's leading online platform for fashion goes beyond the data lake [Internet]. 2020 [cited 2020 Dec 15]. https://www.youtube.com/watch?v=eiUhV56uVUc
10. Cunningham, J.: Netflix Data Mesh: Composable Data Processing - Justin Cunningham [Internet]. 2020 [cited 2020 Sep 25]. https://www.youtube.com/watch?v=TO_IiN06jJ4

Data Shopping — How an Enterprise Data Marketplace Supports Data Democratization in Companies

Rebecca Eichler[1]([⊠]), Christoph Gröger[2], Eva Hoos[2], Holger Schwarz[1],
and Bernhard Mitschang[1]

[1] University of Stuttgart, Universitätsstraße 38, 70569 Stuttgart, Germany
{rebecca.eichler,holger.schwarz,
bernhard.mitschang}@ipvs.uni-stuttgart.de
[2] Robert Bosch GmbH, Borsigstraße 4, 70469 Stuttgart, Germany
{christoph.groeger,eva.hoos}@de.bosch.com

Abstract. To exploit the company's data value, employees must be able to find, understand and access it. The process of making corporate data available to the majority of the company's employees is referred to as data democratization. In this work, we present the current state and challenges of data democratization in companies, derived from a comprehensive literature study and expert interviews we conducted with a manufacturer. In this context a data consumer's journey is presented that reflects the required steps, tool types and roles for finding, understanding and accessing data in addition to revealing three data democratization challenges. To address these challenges we propose the use of an enterprise data marketplace, a novel type of information system for sharing data within the company. We developed a prototype based on which a suitability assessment of a data marketplace yields an improved consumer journey and demonstrates that the marketplace addresses the data democratization challenges and consequently, shows that the marketplace is suited for realizing data democratization.

Keywords: Data marketplace · Data democratization · Data sharing

1 Introduction

The potential of a company's data can only be exploited if its employees can find, access and use it for their respective use cases. However, it has been reported that 60–73% of data in the enterprises remains unused [1]. To address this issue, data democratization has become increasingly relevant [2].

The objective of data democratization is to empower and motivate the majority of company employees to find, understand, access, use and share data across the enterprise, in a secure and compliant way [2–4]. In this sense, Lefebvre et al. [2] define four data democratization dimensions, the first signifies enabling broader access to data and tools, the second, developing data-related and data-analytic skills, e.g., for data cleansing. The third entails the collaboration and knowledge sharing amongst employees, and the fourth

J. De Weerdt and A. Polyvyanyy (Eds.): CAiSE Forum 2022, LNBIP 452, pp. 19–26, 2022.
https://doi.org/10.1007/978-3-031-07481-3_3

comprises the promotion of data value. To assess the current state of data democratization based on these dimensions and investigate the democratization challenges, we conducted a literature study and expert interviews with a globally active manufacturer. In this work, we propose the use of data marketplaces as a platform for addressing the data democratization challenges.

Data Marketplaces are information systems for trading data and data-related services [5, 6]. Their main features include searching, buying and selling of data [6]. These services are offered through a storefront interface where users can shop for data [7]. So far, there is little research on enterprise data marketplaces (EDMP) which enable the exchange of corporate data between employees [7, 8] and thus, directly contribute to the first democratization dimension. However, how an enterprise data marketplace addresses data democratization has not been investigated in detail.

In this respect, we present the following contributions: Based on the literature study and interviews conducted with the manufacturer, we developed *a data consumer's journey* which reflects the steps, the involved roles and current tool types for finding, understanding and accessing data within a company, in Sect. 2. From this journey, we derive *current challenges of data democratization*, also provided in Sect. 2, and present data marketplaces as a possible solution approach. Lastly, we implemented a prototype based on which we asses *the suitability of enterprise data marketplaces* for addressing the data democratization challenges in Sect. 3. Section 4 covers related work and Sect. 5 concludes this paper.

2   Data Democratization - Current State and Challenges

In order to ascertain the current state and challenges of data democratization we conducted a literature study. Some of the research introduces definitions and dimensions of data democratization, yet lack detail on how it is implemented and on the workflows surrounding data [2–4, 9]. Labadie et al. [10] propose data catalogs, data asset inventories with discovery, description and organization functionality, as tools for data democratization, yet it remains unclear how employees gain access to data. Other research provides a rough insight into the current workflows for handling data [3, 11, 12]. To incorporate a practical perspective on workflows for data democratization, we conducted over ten expert interviews with employees of a global manufacturer in various data-related roles, such as data scientists as well as enterprise and solution architects. The manufacturer is active in a variety of sectors like the mobility or industrial sector, and operates a global manufacturing network.

On the basis of the literature study and the expert interviews, we derived a representative consumer journey for industrial enterprises describing how consumers obtain relevant data for their use case. The consumer journey presented in Sect. 2.1 provides insights into the required steps, the involved roles and which tool types are used for finding, understanding and accessing data. Based on this, current challenges in data democratization for data consumers are deduced in Sect. 2.2.

2.1   The Data Consumer Journey

The representative data consumer journey for industrial enterprises, illustrated in Fig. 1, consists of four segments, *finding*, *requesting* and *obtaining access to*, and *preparing* data. Due to lack of space, the data preparation is not discussed here. To illustrate the journey, we exemplify it through a manufacturing engineer who needs maintenance data from production lines, to create a machine maintenance dashboard.

To begin with, data consumers must find relevant data for their use case which involves *searching* for data, *understanding* it and *evaluating* its suitability. In order to use a search function all data must be inventoried through, e.g., a data catalog tool [10]. For example, the engineer searches for "sensor data production line P1" in the catalog to find registered sensor data. The consumer then evaluates the data's relevance based on explanations or metadata. These are provided through metadata management tools like data catalogs, data quality platforms or business glossaries, or by the data owner or domain expert. Amongst others, the metadata includes the business meaning, its provenance, quality and modelling information. Having determined the data's suitability, the consumer continues searching or pursues data access. In continuation of our example, the engineer consults the metadata offered through the data catalog, e.g., explaining that it is data on machine temperatures and thus is relevant for the maintenance dashboard. The engineer gathers additional information on the quality from a data quality platform and term definitions from a business glossary.

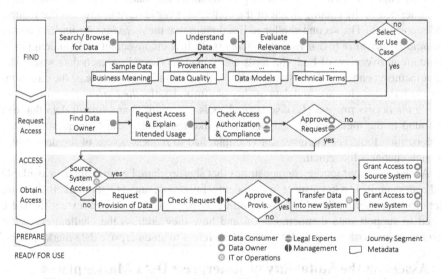

Fig. 1. Data consumer journey in industrial enterprises with involved roles

Gaining access to data entails requesting and obtaining access. Within the first step, the consumer must *find the data owner* and send a *request for access* including the intended usage. This is relevant for compliance to legal regulations such as the General Data Protection Regulation (GDPR). The request is either sent manually, e.g., via email, or through an authorization tool if the tool registers the desired data. The owner or a legal entity then *checks the consumers authorization* based on the data's confidentiality and the employee's clearance level. If either is insufficient the request is declined and the consumer resumes the search. In our example the engineer wants to access data which cannot be requested through the authorization tool, however, the owner is registered in the data catalog and the engineer can send a request through other channels, e.g., email. As the sensor data is not personal data, the engineer may process it for the intended use case and hence, the request is approved by the owner.

Next, the owner or IT specialists determine whether to grant *access to the source system* based on factors such as the system's capacity. If this is not possible the data must be *transferred to another system* like a data lake. The transfer may have to be approved through management, as it can be costly. At this stage, the consumers either resume the search or have gained access to the data. In our example, the engineer is granted access to the source system and can now begin using the data.

2.2 Data Democratization Challenges for Data Consumers

Several data democratization challenges can be derived from the data consumer journey as described above. Firstly, *the process involves several parties (C1)* ranging from the data consumer over the data owner, IT specialists, legal experts and management. With each additional party, the process becomes more complex and time-consuming, as the responsible people have to be found and contacted. In our example scenario, the manufacturing engineer has to locate various persons such as the data owner or domain expert, if not defined in the catalog. Each of the contacted people have to process the request and report back. The second challenge lies therein that the *metadata for understanding the data is spread across a variety of tools (C2)*. It is inconvenient and challenging to maintain an overview of both the tools and metadata viewed on each data asset. The manufacturing engineer, for instance, had to collect metadata from at least the data catalog, the business glossary, and data quality platform. Lastly, *the tools are not integrated across the access process (C3),* so several tools are required and not all data that can be found in the metadata management tools like the catalog can be requested in the authorization tool. The engineer, for example, had to request access of the data owner through channels like email.

As the consumer journey demonstrates that sharing data, i.e., making data available and accessing it, is a key aspect in data democratization, and as data marketplaces are platforms for sharing data [13], we examine in the following to what extent these are suited to support data democratization and how they address the challenges. In the ensuing sections, the term (data) marketplace refers to an enterprise data marketplace.

3   Assessing the Suitability of Enterprise Data Marketplaces for Data Democratization Based on a Marketplace Prototype

In this section, we demonstrate to which extent the EDMP as a platform for trading data within an enterprise [7], supports the consumer journey and solves the challenges (C1–3). To do this, we have developed an EDMP prototype which is built on a microservices architecture and is implemented with the Spring framework[1]. It has a metadata repository

---

[1] https://spring.io/.

realized with a Neo4J[2] database and the metadata is modeled according to our metadata model HANDLE [14]. The enterprise landscape is simulated by a variety of databases and a data lake which are registered in the data catalog Apache Atlas[3]. With regard to functionality, it offers browse and search options with a detailed view for data discovery, service access- and subscription management, service registration for publishing data and license management for data governance.

3.1 The Consumer Journey with an Enterprise Data Marketplace

We conducted a user study in which we recorded the consumers' journeys while using the EDMP prototype. Figure 2 shows the workflow with the marketplace in accordance to the consumer journey as presented in Fig. 1.

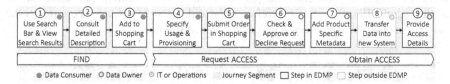

Fig. 2. Workflow of the data consumer journey with an enterprise data marketplace

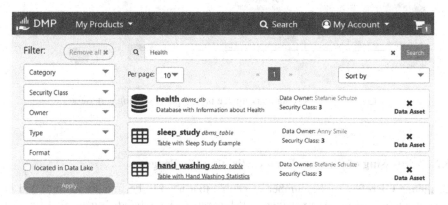

Fig. 3. Enterprise data marketplace prototype – search results

In step 1, the consumer can find and browse through search results as shown in Fig. 3. Clicking on a search result opens a detailed description in step 2, which contains the available metadata on the data to help the consumer understand and evaluate its usefulness. This metadata and the search results are collected from the data catalog. If fitting, the consumer selects the data by adding it to the shopping cart in step 3. In the shopping cart, the intended usage and the desired provisioning are specified and selected

---

[2] https://neo4j.com/.

[3] https://atlas.apache.org/.

for each data set, as displayed in Fig. 4. Requesting access is step 5, by submitting the order in the shopping cart. The request is forwarded automatically to the according data owner, with information on the intended usage, provisioning and information on the consumer such as the clearance level, department etc. The data owner either declines or approves the request in step 6. If not present, the owner is prompted to supply product specific metadata in step 7, such as the license and permitted usage. If necessary the owner must then initiate the process of transferring the data into the data lake or another system in step 8. Meanwhile the consumer can track the current state of the request to see, e.g., if it is being approved, enriched with metadata, transferred into a new system etc. Lastly, the consumer receives access details to the data.

Therefore, the EDMP supports the consumer in the first two journey segments, finding and requesting access. The third segment, obtaining access, is partially supported. Only the request to provision and the realization thereof are not part of the marketplace. It can be seen that most of the consumer journey within industrial enterprises can be carried out through the EDMP and it is therefore improved. How the marketplace supports the journeys in other enterprise types remains to be investigated.

Fig. 4. Enterprise data marketplace prototype - shopping cart view

3.2 Addressing of the Data Democratization Challenges

Challenge C1 refers to the number of people that need to be found and contacted in the consumer process. As explained in [8], companies are building data catalogs, and are assigning data owners to datasets. Our prototype integrates with a catalog, and extracts metadata like the owner, so the consumer does not have to find the relevant people manually. Furthermore, communications such as the access request are sent to the relevant people automatically and the marketplace interface provides participants with a workflow and overview of new, active and expired requests and subscriptions.

The second challenge concerns the distribution of metadata in different tools. The EDMP prototype addresses C2 by integrating these metadata in the detailed description which is accessible through the search mask and references the respective tools.

Lacking integration in the toolchain across the access process is challenge C3. As shown in Sect. 3.1, an EDMP provides support through most of the consumer journeys workflow. Finding data and requesting access are supported in the EDMP. Transferring data into another system, however, is exempt from its capabilities and not supported through an integrated toolchain. Summing up, it has been shown that an enterprise data marketplace addresses the three democratization challenges.

4 Related Work on Data Marketplaces

We have searched for literature on relevant platforms for this topic such as dblp[4] and found out that data marketplaces are studied in both general and specialised contexts. For instance, data marketplace characteristics [15–17], emerging markets, trends [16, 17] and challenges [17] as well as current research fields [5] are identified in research articles. More specialized research focuses on, e.g., data marketplaces for IoT data [18, 19], or the use of specific technologies such as the distributed ledger technology [19, 20]. The listed research provides insights into a wide variety of data marketplace topics, however, not into the specifics of enterprise data marketplaces.

There are few research articles that address enterprise data marketplaces. Among these is research by Fernandez et al. [12] who differentiate internal marketplaces, which are synonymous to enterprise data marketplaces or a report by Wells [7] highlighting characteristics, components, services and involved technologies of such marketplaces and our work [8] in which we underline the need for enterprise data marketplaces. This research does not, however, discuss the enterprise marketplace in the context of data democratization. In contrast, Gröger [3] who presents the marketplace as a central element in the data ecosystem as well as Tata Consultancy Services [21] argue that enterprise data marketplaces are relevant for democratizing data. Yet both do not provide details on how the marketplace supports data democratization. Hence, this article covered this gap in existing literature by examining the democratization challenges and how these are addressed by an enterprise data marketplace.

5 Conclusion

Data democratization with its objective of making data available within the company has become increasingly important. Based on a representative data consumer journey within industrial enterprises, we presented the current state and challenges of data democratization. In this work we proposed the use of an enterprise data marketplace to support data democratization. Our marketplace prototype yields a consumer journey in which the democratization challenges are addressed. Consequently, we have shown that enterprise data marketplaces are a suited approach to foster data democratization in industrial enterprises. In future, we intend to investigate the data provider perspective and further implementation aspects of enterprise data marketplaces.

---

[4] https://dblp.org/.

References

1. Gualtieri, M., et al.: The Forrester Wave: Big Data Hadoop Distributions, Q1 2016. Forrester Res. (2016)
2. Lefebvre, H., Legner, C., Fadler, M.: Data democratization : toward a deeper understanding. In: Proceedings of the International Conference on Information Systems (ICIS) (2021)
3. Gröger, C.: There is no AI without data. Commun. ACM. **64**, 98–108 (2021)
4. Awasthi, P., George, J.: A case for data democratization. In: Proceedings of the 26th Americas Conference on Information Systems (AMCIS) (2020)
5. Lange, J., Stahl, F., Vossen, G.: Datenmarktplätze in verschiedenen Forschungsdisziplinen: Eine Übersicht. Informatik-Spektrum **41**(3), 170–180 (2017). https://doi.org/10.1007/s00287-017-1044-3
6. Meisel, L., Spiekermann, M.: Datenmarktplätze - Plattformen für Datenaustausch und Datenmonetarisierung in der Data Economy. Fraunhofer ISST (2019)
7. Wells, D.: The rise of the data marketplace: data as a service. Eckerson Gr. (2017)
8. Eichler, R., Giebler, C., Gröger, C., Hoos, E., Schwarz, H., Mitschang, B.: Enterprise-wide metadata management: an industry case on the current state and challenges. In: Proceedings of the 24th International Conference on Business Information Systems (BIS), pp. 269–279 (2021)
9. Zeng, J., Glaister, K.W.: Value creation from big data: looking inside the black box. Strateg. Organ. **16**, 105–140 (2018)
10. Labadie, C., Legner, C., Eurich, M., Fadler, M.: FAIR enough? Enhancing the usage of enterprise data with data catalogs. In: Proceedings of the IEEE 22nd Conference on Business Informatics (CBI), pp. 201–210 (2020)
11. Gröger, C., Hoos, E.: Ganzheitliches Metadatenmanagement im Data Lake: Anforderungen, IT-Werkzeuge und Herausforderungen in der Praxis. In: Proceedings of the 18. Fachtagung für Datenbanksysteme für Business, Technologie und Web (BTW) (2019)
12. Fernandez, R.C., Subramaniam, P., Franklin, M.J.: Data market platforms: trading data assets to solve data problems. Proc. VLDB Endow. **13**, 1933–1947 (2020)
13. Spiekermann, M., Tebernum, D., Wenzel, S., Otto, B.: A metadata model for data goods. In: Multikonferenz Wirtschaftsinformatik (MKWI), pp. 326–337 (2018)
14. Eichler, R., Giebler, C., Gröger, C., Schwarz, H., Mitschang, B.: Modeling metadata in data lakes—a generic model. Data Knowl. Eng. **136**, 101931 (2021)
15. Schomm, F., Stahl, F., Vossen, G.: Marketplaces for data: an initial survey. ACM SIGMOD Rec. **42**, 15–26 (2013)
16. Stahl, F., Schomm, F., Vomfell, L., Vossen, G.: Marketplaces for digital data: Quo Vadis? Comput. Inf. Sci. **10**, 22 (2017)
17. Spiekermann, M.: Data marketplaces: trends and monetisation of data goods. Intereconomics **54**(4), 208–216 (2019). https://doi.org/10.1007/s10272-019-0826-z
18. Zheng, Z., Mao, W., Wu, F., Chen, G.: Challenges and opportunities in IoT data markets. In: Proceedings of the 4th International Workshop on Social Sensing (SocialSense), pp. 1–2 (2019)
19. Ramachandran, G.S., Radhakrishnan, R., Krishnamachari, B.: Towards a decentralized data marketplace for smart cities. In: Proceedings of the IEEE International Smart Cities Conference (ISC2), pp. 1–8 (2018)
20. Roman, D., Stefano, G.: Towards a reference architecture for trusted data marketplaces: the credit scoring perspective. In: Proceedings of the 2nd International Conference on Open and Big Data (OBD), pp. 95–101. IEEE (2016)
21. Saxena, S.: Enterprise data marketplace: democratizing data within organizations. Tata Consultancy Services (2018)

An Ontological Characterization of a Conceptual Model of the Human Genome

Alberto García S[1]([✉])(iD), Giancarlo Guizzardi[2,3](iD), Oscar Pastor[1](iD),
Veda C. Storey[4](iD), and Anna Bernasconi[1,5](iD)

[1] Universitat Politècnica de València, Valencia, Spain
{algarsi3,opastor}@pros.upv.es
[2] Free University of Bozen-Bolzano, Bolzano, Italy
Giancarlo.Guizzardi@unibz.it
[3] University of Twente, Twente, The Netherlands
g.guizzardi@utwente.nl
[4] Georgia State University, Atlanta, GA, USA
vstorey@gsu.edu
[5] Politecnico di Milano, Milan, Italy
anna.bernasconi@polimi.it

Abstract. The ability to sequence the human genome is a scientific, historical breakthrough. Although the human genome mapping is available to all scientists, information about it can be difficult to share. The Conceptual Schema of the Human Genome represents the concepts required to holistically understand the human genome. We report on our continued efforts to ensure that the human genome can be meaningfully shared by conducting an ontological analysis and enrichment of the conceptual model to facilitate domain understanding and data exchange among heterogeneous systems. The analysis and enrichment process is supported by the ontology-driven conceptual modeling language, OntoUML, to gain ontological clarity and demonstrated on a relevant section of the Pathways view of the schema. Consistent with the overall objective of designing a sound genomics information system, the results lead to major modeling implications for the: characterization of biological entities; changes in biological entities over time; and representation of chemical compounds. Our research shows that the inclusion of a strong ontological foundation in a conceptual model contributes to the design of complex systems.

Keywords: Ontological analysis · Conceptual schema of the human genome · Ontological foundation · Heterogeneous data representation

1   Introduction

The modeling of the human genome is a fascinating and extremely important area of research due to its potential to impact all of mankind through improved

J. De Weerdt and A. Polyvyanyy (Eds.): CAiSE Forum 2022, LNBIP 452, pp. 27–35, 2022.
https://doi.org/10.1007/978-3-031-07481-3_4

treatments and possibly, removal of diseases. In essence, this modeling is contributing to understanding life itself. Progressing research on the human genome, however, is challenged for many reasons, perhaps the greatest of which is the fact that the body of knowledge surrounding the human genome constantly changes and evolves as scientists and researchers all over the world work with it. Furthermore, the terminology and concepts employed in genomics can be imprecise and change continuously. So does the scope and complexity of the modeling required to represent them. The definitions of terms needed to characterize any phenomena rely on the experience of the domain experts who use and interpret them. Definitions may be purposely abstract to reflect the limited, and constantly changing, knowledge of the domain. They cannot simply be translated into an unambiguous representation of knowledge. However, a fundamental prerequisite for analyzing and understanding any complex domain, is to facilitate a shared understanding among the people who work in that domain.

The most common artifacts used for representing concepts are lightweight ontologies (logical specifications in a form of Description Logics) and thesauruses of controlled vocabulary [15], because they provide standard concepts and definitions. However, they can only correctly represent a minor portion of relevant facts in genomics [4]. Conceptual models are appropriate because they facilitate the exchange of information [13], while providing a sound basis to make a conceptualization process explicit and facilitate a shared understanding of a domain [11]. For the human genome domain, applying conceptual modeling can: improve communication among physicians, geneticists, biologists, and other researchers; assist in knowledge transfer; and, ultimately, enable efficient exploitation of information for progressing the understanding of the human genome [12].

Prior research has created a Conceptual Schema of the Human Genome (CSHG) [2]. This research extends the conceptual model by making the definition of the relevant concepts precise, explicit and understandable. We conduct an ontological analysis and enrichment of the Pathways view of the current model. We use "ontological" in a strong sense. Our analysis aims at revealing and explicitly modeling aspects related to the *nature* and *real-world semantics* of entity types and relations by employing the conceptual modeling language OntoUML [5], which is grounded in the Unified Foundational Ontology (UFO) [7]. The contribution is to reformulate the conceptual model, showing how a foundational ontology brings ontological clarity to complex models by facilitating domain understanding and data exchange among heterogeneous systems [6].

2 Conceptual Schema of the Genome (CSHG)

The Conceptual Schema of the Human Genome (CSHG) [3] focused on representing the most relevant concepts of genomics. Creating this holistic schema required the integration of conceptual components that represent the relevant data that connect the genome structure (genotype) with its expression of real world behavior (phenotype). Evolution of the CSHG resulted in five views: structural, variation, transcription, proteome, bibliography, and pathway. Using conceptual views allows us to focus on specific dimensions of interest, which have many practical uses such as identifying and managing genomic variations related to the treatment of Alzheimer's [9], developing a conceptual model-based framework to improve data quality processes for precision medicine [10], of reporting early diagnosis of alcohol sensitivity [14].

Here, we focus on the Pathways view, which describes the chemical reactions that explain the different molecular processes. This view reflects very critical aspects of the genomics domain, including a *biological event* that addresses how genome elements interact to produce a biological behavior. Given its importance and richness, this view provides an appropriate way to motivate and demonstrate the need for the type of analysis and redesign proposed here. A portion of the Pathways view is depicted in Fig. 1 as a UML class diagram. The model is centered on the notions of entity and event, represented by homonymous classes.

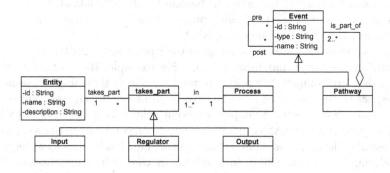

Fig. 1. Subset of selected classes from the pathways view of the CSHG

Consistent with the terminology of geneticists, an entity class identifies any possible physical component present in a body and plays a role in an event. In turn, an event class represents the biological events that occur in a body. Events are recursively composed of additional events. An event can be a pathway (complex event, made up of other events) or a process (elementary event). A process is then an atomic, simple event of a given type. A pathway is a more complex type of event that is decomposed into a specific set of events (processes or pathways). A process is a specific interaction between entities. An entity can participate as an input, an output, or a regulator. These associated sets of inputs, outputs, and (optionally) regulators characterize the process functionality. When an entity takes part in a specific process, it assumes one of these three roles.

3   OntoUML

OntoUML is an ontology-driven conceptual modeling language based on the upper ontology Unified Foundational Ontology (UFO, [5,7]). OntoUML uses stereotypes to represent the mapping between its modeling constructs and UFO ontological categories. OntoUML is built upon the fundamental distinction between Types and Individuals. Types are patterns of features that are repeatable across multiple instances. OntoUML includes a theory of higher-order types so first-order types are types instantiated by individuals, whereas higher-order types (represented by the stereotype TYPE) are instantiated by other types. UFO countenances two fundamental types of individuals: endurants (objects and their existentially dependent reified aspects) and perdurants (events and processes).

Endurants types are classified on two dimensions, sortality (identity) and rigidity. Sortals are types whose instances obey a single identity principle (all of the same KIND); non-sortals are types that classify instances of multiple kinds. A type is rigid if it defines essential characteristics of its instances; anti-rigid if it defines contingent characteristics for all instances. The type person is rigid, but student is anti-rigid. Kinds represent the genuine fundamental types of objects that exist according to a particular conceptualization of a domain. All objects belong to exactly one kind. There can be other static specializations of a kind, namely SUBKINDS; e.g., the kind "gene product" can be specialized into the subkinds "coding RNA" and "non-coding RNA".

Objects can be classified depending on their principle of unity, i.e., the principle binding the parts that form a whole. For example, they can be COLLECTIVES if they are composed of parts (termed *members*) that play the same role with respect to the whole, or FUNCTIONAL COMPLEXES if they are composed of parts (termed *components*) that play different roles with respect to the whole. Finally, objects can be QUANTITIES to represent homeomerous entities (i.e., entities repeatably decomposable into entities of the same kind), such as water, sand, or blood. Since most of the kinds in a domain are those whose instances are functional complexes, we use the stereotype KIND simply to represent them.

Anti-Rigid types are specialized into PHASES and ROLES. Both phases and roles are dynamic types. Phases have intrinsic dynamic classification conditions, i.e., they capture a cluster of change conditions in intrinsic properties. Roles, in contrast, have relational dynamic classification conditions, i.e., they capture a cluster of change conditions bound to changes in a relational context. For instance, a blood cell has multiple phases such as blood stem cell, red blood cell, etc. depending on its maturity (i.e., an intrinsic property). In the case of roles, a person (i.e., an instance of the kind person) can be a patient (role) while participating in a medical treatment.

Phases and Roles are sortals (classify things of the same kind). We can, however, have analogous anti-rigid non-sortal classes, namely, PHASEMIXINS and ROLEMIXINS. As non-sortals, phaseMixins and roleMixins classify instances of multiple kinds. For instance, suppose a protein (kind) and an organic chemical compound (kind) play the role of a regulator in a specific biological process. There are two different roles: the "regulator protein" and the "regulator chemical compound". Both regulate a process so we can abstract them into a new roleMixin, called regulator, from which the other two roles specialize. PhaseMixins and RoleMixins can be thought as refactoring classes (abstracting properties common to entities of multiple kinds) and, hence, they are always *abstract* types (i.e., types that cannot be directly instantiated). We can have refactoring (non-sortal) types that are rigid, i.e., that abstract *essential* properties common to entities of several kinds. These are marked as the CATEGORY stereotype.

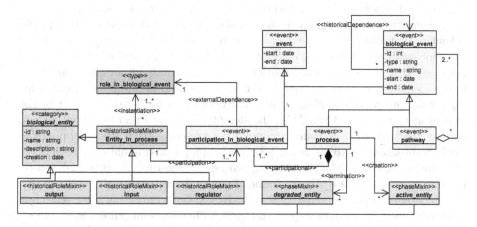

Fig. 2. Ontologically enriched version of the analyzed concepts.

Objects bear a number of *aspects*, some of which are intrinsic (existentially depend solely on them): QUALITIES or MODES. Qualities can be directly associated with structured value spaces (e.g., color or temperature); MODES are full-fledged object-like entities with their own aspects but still existentially dependent on some bearer. Besides intrinsic aspects, are relational ones: entities that are existentially dependent on a multitude of individuals, binding them. These are RELATORS, which are the truth-makers of material relations. For instance, the "participation in trial" relator connects a patient with a clinical trial.

OntoUML has perdurants to represent events [1]. Events are characterized with the «event» stereotype. They have their own properties and can be decomposed. Events are immutable because they only exist in the past. Endurants and perdurants interact in several ways. For example, endurants *participate* in events, are *created* by events, and are *terminated* by events. Finally, since events are particularized instances that only exist in the past, roles played by objects in an event (i.e., while an event was occurring) are termed HISTORICAL ROLES (or HISTORICAL ROLE MIXINS, depending whether they are sortals).

4   Ontological Analysis and Redesign

We review the original conceptualization underlying CSHG using an ontological analysis mediated by OntoUML. The results lead to an improved CSHG, whose sound and precise ontological commitment fulfills a conceptual clarification (Fig. 2). This analysis focuses on clarifying the notions of entity and event and how they relate to each other. The conceptual characterization of the Pathways view of the CSHG begins with the identification of its two main concepts, "entity" and "event". In the original UML class diagram of Fig. 1, are represented as simple classes. However, their exact conceptual characterization can be made explicit using OntoUML's finer-grained class and association constructs (reflecting UFO's distinctions among endurant and event types and relations).

The entity concept (renamed "biological entity") is used to define every physical entity that may have a role in one or more processes. Therefore, we annotated the concept of entity and the concept of simple with the «category» stereotype because categories aggregate essential properties to individuals that follow different identity principles (belong to different kinds). The "event" concept helps represent the set of biological events that occur in a body and are part of the human metabolism. In OntoUML, the stereotype «event» represents ontological entities that unfold over time, accumulating temporal parts and mapping the world from situation to situation [1]. By mapping our original class "event" to that notion in OntoUML [1], we add two new attributes, «begin» and «end», because events in OntoUML are framed by specific time intervals.

The original model had one type-reflexive relation connecting the Event class with itself and the rolenames "pre" and "post". That modeling choice left ambiguous whether this relation represented a mere temporal precedence between occurrences or a stronger causal connection. To make it explicit that the intended semantics referred to the latter, we used OntoUML's «historicalDependence» stereotype [1]. If an event of type A is historically dependent on a event of type B, then instances of A must necessarily be preceded by instances of type B. Historical dependence implies temporal precedence, but not vice versa.

Events can be composed of a set of other events, forming partonomies. This can be illuminated by the mereology of events underlying OntoUML [8]. Mereology accounts for two orthogonal dimensions of decomposition of events: a *structural dimension* and a *participation dimension*. For CSHG, following the structural dimension, there are two types of events: the process and the pathway. A process is an atomic, simple event of a given type that can not be decomposed into smaller parts, whereas a pathway is a complex event that can be decomposed into smaller events, which are either processes or pathways. This dimension is represented through an aggregation relationship with the event class. Following the language's imposed mereological theory, complex entities must be composed of at least two disjoint parts (the *Weak Supplementation Axiom* [8]) with minimum cardinality constraints on the relations. This revised part of the model is a direct instantiation of UFO's structural partonomy pattern [8].

The participation dimension is characterized by representing the role that biological entities play in processes. This was originally modeled by the "takes_part" class in the UML schema, where we showed that an entity can act as an input, an output, or a regulator in a process. This representation has been expanded in the OntoUML version of the schema. First, we created a set of classes stereotyped with «historicalRoleMixin» to indicate playing roles, which biological entities have participated in, as an event. Unlike the UML schema, the minimum cardinality of the association between the historical role and the process is one. For a biological entity to play the role, it must have mandatorily participated in an event. Historical roles explicitly describe the variety of roles that biological entities may play in the processes.

Events depend on biological entities. Since atomic events (i.e., processes) are directly existentially dependent on biological entities, we can use the extensionality principle of the event mereology to derive the existential dependency of complex processes. The defined role mixins enables the creation of "portions" to describe the specific participation of an entity. The participation class, stereotyped as «event», divides an event into the individual participation of biological entities. Every instance of the "participation" class is derived from parthood and existential dependence, and bound to a specific subtype of a historical role mixin. Making explicit the notion of participation is of great importance from an ontological point of view. For instance, the process by which proteins are synthesized (translation) can be decomposed into atomic steps (e.g., initiation, elongation, and termination) to model the "constructed" dimension by creating segments using temporal schemes as external references. It can also be decomposed into portions that encapsulate the participation of biological entities in the whole process (e.g., participation of the ribosome and the mRNA strand).

Another capability, enabled by the use of the «event» stereotype, is modeling the creation and termination of biological entities. Millions of molecules are created and destroyed by different events that occur in our body, which is a special type of participation of endurants (i.e., biological entities) in events. To represent this situation, we modeled two phases to represent whether an entity exists or has been destroyed. The «phaseMixin» stereotype is used to represent changes in intrinsic properties of kinds (destroyed or not). If a biological entity is related to an event using an association stereotyped with «creation», that entity is created in that event. Similarly, for the «termination» stereotype.

5   Results

Several changes resulted from the ontological analysis, the most important of which is the clarification that enforces conceptual transparency on the initial representation. The ontological analysis identified and changed several aspects of the model to better grasp domain semantics, improving the representation of events and how biological entities change over time. The use of the «phase» stereotype in the OntoUML model enriches the representation of the effects caused by events. In the UML version, an entity can act as an input, an output, or a regulator. In the OntoUML version, an additional dimension allows us to indicate whether the entity has been degraded. An entity can be modeled that is: i) degraded as a result of a process; ii) created as a result of a process; iii) modified as a result of a process; or iv) degraded as a result of regulating a process. This change in the state of an entity (degraded or not) could not be modeled without the phase stereotype. This clarifies that the changes of biological entities in our bodies result from processes, but it is not clear how to model the degradation of entities within the UML model. The creation of the active_entity and degraded_entity phases provides additional mechanisms to ensure the correctness of the model. This prevents introducing errors when instantiating and populating the model. Such constraints are difficult to identify in the UML model.

6 Conclusion

The modeling of the human genome is an effort to understand life through the development of a conceptual model. This research has several implications. First, recognizing the complexity of this domain shows the importance of representing the human genome by a model that supports a shared understanding. Second, by making the ontological clarity of the conceptual model explicit, it is possible for the model to have a solid foundation. Further work will include the addition of notions of situation and disposition. These concepts are important because they enable the representation of diseases and pathways using situations and altered functions of modified proteins as dispositions. Various parts of CSHG will be instantiated and the ontological exercise applied to the remaining views. Thus, conceptual models are a practical way for domain experts and computer scientists to share the knowledge needed to develop systems to support processing of the huge amount of genomics data that now exists.

References

1. Almeida, J.P.A., Falbo, R.A., Guizzardi, G.: Events as entities in ontology-driven conceptual modeling. In: Laender, A.H.F., Pernici, B., Lim, E.-P., de Oliveira, J.P.M. (eds.) ER 2019. LNCS, vol. 11788, pp. 469–483. Springer, Cham (2019). https://doi.org/10.1007/978-3-030-33223-5_39
2. García, A., et al.: Towards the understanding of the human genome: a holistic conceptual modeling approach. IEEE Access **8**, 197111–197123 (2020)
3. García, A., et al.: A Conceptual Model-based approach to improve the representation and management of omics data in Precision Medicine. IEEE Access **9**, 154071–154085 (2021)
4. Gaudet, P., et al.: Gene ontology: pitfalls, biases, and remedies. In: The gene ontology handbook, pp. 189–205. Humana Press, New York (2017)
5. Guizzardi, G.: Ontological Foundations for Structural Conceptual Models. Ph.D. thesis, University of Twente, January 2005
6. Guizzardi, G., Bernasconi, A., Pastor, O., Storey, V.C.: Ontological unpacking as explanation: the case of the viral conceptual model. In: Ghose, A., Horkoff, J., Silva Souza, V.E., Parsons, J., Evermann, J. (eds.) ER 2021. LNCS, vol. 13011, pp. 356–366. Springer, Cham (2021). https://doi.org/10.1007/978-3-030-89022-3_28
7. Guizzardi, G., et al.: Towards ontological foundations for conceptual modeling: the unified foundational ontology (UFO) story. Appl. Ontology **10**(3–4), 259–271 (2015)
8. Guizzardi, G., Wagner, G., de Almeida Falbo, R., Guizzardi, R.S.S., Almeida, J.P.A.: Towards ontological foundations for the conceptual modeling of events. In: Ng, W., Storey, V.C., Trujillo, J.C. (eds.) ER 2013. LNCS, vol. 8217, pp. 327–341. Springer, Heidelberg (2013). https://doi.org/10.1007/978-3-642-41924-9_27

9. Palacio, A.L., et al.: Genomic information systems applied to precision medicine: genomic data management for Alzheimer's disease treatment. In: International Conference on Information Systems Development (2018)

10. Palacio, A.L., et al.: Toward an effective medicine of precision by using conceptual modelling of the genome. In: IEEE/ACM International Workshop on Software Engineering in Healthcare Systems, pp. 14–17 (2018)

11. Pastor, O.: Conceptual modeling of life: beyond the homo sapiens. In: Comyn-Wattiau, I., Tanaka, K., Song, I.-Y., Yamamoto, S., Saeki, M. (eds.) ER 2016. LNCS, vol. 9974, pp. 18–31. Springer, Cham (2016). https://doi.org/10.1007/978-3-319-46397-1_2

12. Pastor, O., et al.: Using conceptual modeling to improve genome data management. Briefings Bioinf. **22**(1), 45–54 (2021)

13. Pastor, O., et al.: Model-driven architecture in practice: a software production environment based on conceptual modeling. Springer, Berlin (2007). https://doi.org/10.1007/978-3-540-71868-0

14. Román, J.F.R., et al.: Use of GeIS for early diagnosis of alcohol sensitivity. In: Bioinformatics 2016, pp. 284–289 (2016)

15. Smith, B., et al.: The ontology of the gene ontology. In: AMIA Annual Symposium Proceedings, vol. 2003, p. 609. American Medical Informatics Association (2003)

Synthesizing Configuration Tactics
for Exercising Hidden Options
in Serverless Systems

Jörn Kuhlenkamp, Sebastian Werner[(✉)], Chin Hong Tran, and Stefan Tai

Information Systems Engineering,
Technische Universität Berlin, Berlin, Germany
{jk,sw,ct,st}@ise.tu-berlin.de

Abstract. A proper configuration of an information system can ensure accuracy and efficiency, among other system objectives. Conversely, a poor configuration can have a significant negative impact on the system's performance, reliability, and cost. Serverless systems in particular, which are comprised of many functions and managed services, can quickly risky the danger of misconfiguration, with many provider- and platform-specific, often intransparent and 'hidden' settings. In this paper, we argue to pay close attention to the configuration of serverless systems to exercise options with known accuracy, cost and time. Based on a literature study and long-term serverless systems development experience, we present nine tactics to unlock potentially neglected and unknown options in serverless systems.

Keywords: Serverless system · Configuration methods · Design tactics

1 Introduction

Serverless computing is a new cloud provisioning model appealing to cloud consumers due to increased automation of operational tasks, instant scalability with incoming workload, and no costs for idle computing resources. Consequently, serverless computing promises developers the means for delivering more features for applications in shorter lead times at a lower cost [16].

In the serverless programming model [9], developers build serverless systems as event-driven compositions of (cloud) functions and additional, managed cloud services, such as object storage, messaging queues, and databases. Cloud functions run in a Function-as-a-Service platform such as AWS Lambda, Google Cloud Functions, or Apache OpenWhisk. However, academia and industry report that client-side quality in terms of performance, reliability, and execution costs frequently and significantly mismatches developers' expectations due to poor configurations [14,15] making ignoring configuration particularly risky.

Ironically, configuring serverless systems "accurately" requires developers to understand a cloud platform's quality-sensitive configuration options hidden by the programming model's high abstraction. To this end, related work proposes

J. De Weerdt and A. Polyvyanyy (Eds.): CAiSE Forum 2022, LNBIP 452, pp. 36–44, 2022.
https://doi.org/10.1007/978-3-031-07481-3_5

configuration methods [2,6,8,18]. However, these configuration methods may not live up to developers' expectations, as they focus on accuracy but tend to neglect required cost and time. Furthermore, accuracy with these methods typically depends on implicit assumptions regarding a system's architecture and deployment environment. We find it not convincing to assume that developers that select the serverless computing paradigm to leverage cost and lead-time benefits buy into a configuration approach that demands unknown cost and time investments.

In this context, we define the research question: **How can developers configure serverless systems with predictable accuracy, cost, and time?** Towards this, we present two contributions, (i) a literature review that indicates that accuracy, cost and time of (current) configuration methods are too in-transparent, and (ii) nine tactics for designing future configuration methods with known accuracy, cost and time effectively synthesizing the state-of-the-art.

2 Configuration Fundamentals

Through introducing fundamentals of system configuration methods', we lay the foundation for reviewing existing related work (Sect. 3), introducing **tasks**, and **quality dimensions**, see also Fig. 1.

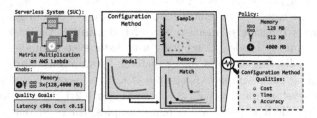

Fig. 1. Exemplary configuration method on Lambda (https://github.com/tawalaya/cat-sizer).

Table 1. Comparison of configuration methods.

	Memory	Batch	Fusion	Placement	Concurrency	Bounds	Weights	Isolated	Chain	Complex
Saha [18]	✓	–	–	–	–	–	–	✓	–	–
Christoforou [5]	✓	✓	–	–	✓	–	–	✓	–	–
Ali [3]	–	✓	–	–	–	✓	–	✓	–	–
Elgamal [8]	✓	–	✓	✓	–	✓	–	✓	✓	✓
Schuler [21]	–	–	–	–	✓	–	–	✓	–	–
Akhtar [2]	✓	–	–	✓	–	✓	–	✓	✓	–
Tariq [24]	–	–	–	–	✓	✓	–	✓	✓	✓
Sánchez-A. [19]	–	–	–	–	✓	✓	–	–	–	✓
Eismann [7]	✓	–	–	–	–	–	✓	✓	–	–
Sedefouglu [22]	✓	–	–	–	–	–	–	✓	–	–
First-Author	Knob					Goal		Composition		

2.1 Tasks

Developers configure systems to meet quality goals. To that extent, a configuration method takes as input a *system under configuration* (SUC), knobs, e.g., a configuration parameter, and goals, e.g., a target throughput, and outputs a policy, e.g., a set of configuration parameters that should meet desired goals. In Fig. 1, we show a running example of sizing "memory" for three functions implementing matrix multiplication on AWS Lambda, with two goals: client-side request-response latency below 90 s and marginal execution cost below 0.1 USD.

To meet both goals, a configuration methods needs to find values for *knob*s, e.g., the memory size of the three functions in our example. A SUC can expose knobs on the platform- or application-level. However, application-level knobs often require developers to modify code, e.g., changing libraries or the function composition. With increasing maturity, a platform typically assimilates relevant application-level knobs to expose them as a feature to foster accessibility [25].

A *goal* is an expression of a developer's preferences for a system quality, e.g., a target latency range. Note that configuration methods assume that a SUC allows observing system qualities included in the goals. A **configuration method** comprises three high-level tasks: *match*, *model*, and *sample* resulting in a *policy* that fits a *goal*. **Matching** finds a policy that fits provided goals accurately. Thus, matching requires searching all possible configurations. To assess how accurately a policy matches goals, matching uses a *system quality model* that captures the cause-effect relationship between a policy and goals, e.g., cost and latency as a function of memory size. **Modelling** is the task of creating such a system quality model. Computing a realistic system quality model typically requires collecting samples under realistic assumptions. **Sampling** is the task of obtaining such samples. A sample is a data record including a policy and measured system quality, e.g., 8 s latency and 0.2 USD cost for 1024 MB memory size. While it is possible to create samples using different approaches, reliable results require experimentation, i.e., making observations on a SUC in a controlled environment.

2.2 Quality Dimensions

Quality dimensions quantify a configuration method's quality, and are hence not to confuse with system qualities used in specifying goals. In order to compare and evaluate configuration methods, we present the three most relevant configuration method qualities in detail.

Accuracy (A) quantifies how closely a configuration method's computed policys fit goals. Goals including multiple system qualities typically require an aggregation function such as a weighted distances function for comparison. Another aspect is stability, which describes the ability of a configuration method to generalize, i.e., maintaining accuracy for changing SUCs. **Costs (C)** comprises all monetary costs for executing a configuration method. It is vital to evaluate not only matching cost but also the modelling and sampling cost. Otherwise, a configuration method implicitly claims that system quality models are reusable and generalize well over arbitrary SUCs. **Time (T)** is the difference between applying a computed policy and starting a configuration method. A configuration method that is fully automated through a configuration system typically allows to easily quantify time for configuration requests. Time for all tasks is relevant because a configuration method can cache samples and system quality models.

3   Literature Review

Building on Sect. 2, we analyse existing proposals for configuring serverless systems in a structured literature review (SLR) [12], extending the scope of serverless computing's literature reviews on other topics [13,17,20,23]. We seed our search for publications in existing serverless computing literature datasets [13,20] including only scientific publications from the years 2018–2021. Each publication includes at least one configuration method in the context of serverless computing. Table 1 summarizes the final set of publications [2,3,5,7,8,18,19,21] in chronological order of appearance.

3.1   Results

SUC. A single client's event typically triggers the execution of multiple downstream functions that form a function composition. We differentiate between approaches for *isolated* functions [3,7,18,22], function *chains* [2,8], and *complex* compositions [5]. While a function chain executes multiple functions sequentially, a complex composition includes switching and parallel executions. Approaches that configure functions in isolation and neglect the composition logic are inclined to propose solutions that do not closely match goals. Complex compositions include perfectly parallelizable execution flows. Some proposals are tightly coupled to a specific system,e.g., [19] is tightly coupled to the concrete implementation of serverless sorting and [21] to the KNative platform [11] hurting general applicability of approaches. First standalone configuration systems begin to emerge, i.e., Tariq et al. [24] provide a middleware called Sequoia for their matching algorithm. Such approaches seems promising because they make fewer assumptions on a SUCs software and deployment architecture.

Knobs. Related work addresses five classes of knobs: memory, batch, fusion, placement, and concurrency. The *memory* knob universally represents setting computing resources for a function (sizing) [2,5,7,8,18,22]. Some approaches use small domain size [7,22] hiding platform options. The *batch* knob comes in the two variants event baching and input batching. *Event batching* [3] collects multiple events before sending them to a single slot, i.e., VM or container. *Input batching* [5] collects various inputs in a single event before execution in a single slot. The *fusion* knob [8] merges a set of function handlers into a single one. In contrast, the *placement* [2,8] knob sets the target deployment environment of a function, e.g., a data center and edge location. Finally, the *concurrency* knob determines the number of events that a function executes in parallel, including two variants. *Function concurrency* [5, 24] determines the sum of events that all slots can process at the same time. *Slot concurrency* [21] determines the number of events that a single slot can process concurrently, i.e., similarly to multi-threading.

Goals. From a developer's perspective, all tuning knobs can influence multiple system qualities, including execution latency, cost, and reliability, but existing proposals commonly focus on a subset of these qualities including throughput [21], execution latency [2, 3, 5, 7, 8, 18, 19, 22], execution cost [2, 3, 5, 7, 8, 22], and reliability [24]. Absolute quality bounds [2, 8, 22] and relative quality weights [7] are both usefully means for expressing developer's quality preferences that are not considered in combination. Hence, we argue that approaches (currently) limit developers' ability to express quality preferences holistically.

Quality Dimensions. Not all proposals explicitly discuss quality dimensions [18]. Multiple proposals evaluate accuracy without cost and time [3, 5, 8, 19, 21]. For example, [5] report high accuracy by quantitative comparisons with an exhaustive search. We argue that extensive sampling and profiling implies high cost [3], and potentially time [5]. Schuler et al. [21] use reinforcement learning that requires 150–600 iterations to stabilize in a policy. For sampling, each iteration executes 500 requests in flight for 30 s. Hence, we infer a stabilization time between 75 min and 5 h and cost of stabilization time multiplied by average throughput. Tarek et al. [8] propose the knob function fusion that implies changing the application logic of a SUC, which makes estimating cost and time of the approach difficult. Most proposals do not discuss how they handle changes to a SUC. Akhtar et al. [2] generate separate quality models for individual functions using Bayesian optimization, and, in a next step, find a suitable configuration for a function chain leveraging Integer Linear Programming. Notably, modelling only requires 5–15 samples. In contrast, Eismann et al. [7] require significant ex-ante sampling and modelling enabling quick matching at the risk of reduced accuracy under system changes.

3.2 Discussion

Configuration promises matching an information system's quality goals accurately at a cost and time investment. To that extent, configuration methods employ three tasks sampling, modeling, and matching. However, configuration methods can significantly differ in (i) when and how they execute each task and (ii) supported knobs, system qualities, and goals. The fundamental design decisions that make up each configuration method are typically justified by improving accuracy or reducing the time or cost of configuration. However, our review indicates that design decisions' negative impacts on other configuration method qualities are often hidden. This predominantly manifests in two ways. First, shifting negative impacts to other tasks. For example, reporting low costs and time for matching at the expense of increased cost and time for sampling and modeling. Second, making specific assumptions about the configured serverless system. For example, assuming a specific workload, function composition, or FaaS platform feature to reduce efforts for sampling and modeling.

Therefore, we believe that it is beneficial to make more explicit the tradeoffs between accuracy, time, and cost that are hidden in the design decisions of current configuration methods. In this way, tradeoffs and assumptions for a configuration method as a whole and for individual design decisions become known to researchers and practitioners, promoting (re)usability. To this end, we propose a modular approach that allows the design decisions of different configuration methods to be combined to meet the requirements of a particular system context. As a first step in this new direction, we propose the use of tactics, which we present in the next section.

4   Tactics

This section presents nine concrete tactics for engineering the quality dimensions of configuration methods. While closely related to design patterns, we rely on the word "tactic" because they are not exclusively usable in configuration systems but also in semi-automated or manual configuration methods. We group the tactics into platform-, knob-, and application-centric tactics. We use a shorthand notation to indicate a tactic's impacts on quality dimensions: accuracy (**A**), cost (**C**), and time (**T**).

Platform-centric Tactics. Platform-centric tactics leverage idiosyncrasies of serverless platforms to improve a configuration method.

T1 - Isolate Executions. Processing multiple events concurrently in the same slot/runtime can significantly impact accuracy (**A**) per event by adding noise to each collected sample, thus, requiring a large number of runs to filter out this noise. Therefore, this tactic assumes that a slot only performs a single (isolated) execution at a time. A correct assumption can reduce the number of runs (**C**, **T**) without sacrificing accuracy (**A**); however, a false assumption runs the danger of reducing accuracy. We observed that several FaaS platforms fulfil the assumptions of this tactic [1,15].

T2 - Automate Operational Tasks. Different runs, i.e., observations, require changing the deployment and configuration of a serverless system. This tactic uses a FaaS platform's capabilities to automate associated operational tasks. Different FaaS platforms require a few seconds to minutes to converge to a new target deployment [14]. If a deployment change converges quickly, the lag between runs shortens, reducing the overall time for sampling (**T**). As a downside, clients can temporarily observe inconsistent deployments in specific FaaS platforms [14]. Not accounting for this behaviour risks of mixing samples (**A**).

T3 - Manifold Testbeds. This tactic uses a FaaS platform's ability to scale multiple deployments independently and isolated with incoming events. Thus, on these platforms, we can deploy policy-variants in parallel and conduct multiple runs simultaneously, similar to Joyner et al. [10]. A potential benefit is reducing the overall time of experimentation (**T**) without increasing costs (**C**) due to serverless platforms' common work-based billing model. However, a FaaS platform's default limits, e.g., regarding the maximum number of concurrent executions, as well as cold-starts, can result in runtime bottlenecks and misleading observations impairing accuracy (**A**).

Knob-centric Tactics. Knob-centric tactics leverage knowledge on the relationship between a knob and its impact on quality to reduce runs while maintaining high accuracy (**A**).

T4 - Constant Quality Function. This tactic assumes that a system's quality does not significantly change for different values of a knob. A configuration method can exploit this behaviour by randomly selecting a value for the knob and thus omitting runs. This assumption typically holds for multiple knobs exposed by FaaS platforms. For example, configuring *functions-tags* never impacts system qualities such as latency. Thus, omitting these knobs when considering new configuration options reduces the time (**T**) and cost (**C**). However, validation of these assumptions is critical to avoid system quality degradation.

T5 - Monotonic Quality Function. This tactic assumes that values of a knob's domain have an inherent order, that quality changes with this order monotonically, and that a configuration method supports bounds in the goal definition. The method can exploit this knowledge by omitting runs after observing quality outside of a predefined bound without reducing accuracy (**A**). While this tactic can reduce cost (**C**), it implies that runs execute sequentially, making this tactic mutually exclusive with (**T3**). For example, all elements in the domain of the `memory` knob are ordered based on their numeric value. For some applications, latency will decrease monotonically for larger memory values. Alternatively, if a predefined quality bound states that end-to-end latency must be smaller than 1 s, a method can omit runs for all smaller memory values after observing a run with a latency over 1 s.

T6 - Quality Function Type. This tactic assumes that quality is a function of a knob's values that follows a known function type, e.g., a linear or an exponential function. A configuration method can exploit this by not observing a SUC under all possible values of a knob's domain but only estimating the parameters of the known function type, which is typically possible using observations from fewer runs. For example, Akhtar et al. [2] assume that execution latency as a function of `memory` follows an exponential decay function.

T7 - Quality Function. This tactic assumes that the function type (see **T6**), including all its parameters, are known. Consequently, a configuration method can omit runs because the relationship between a knob and quality is known already. In other words, this tactic (re-)uses an existing quality model entirely, omitting the tasks sampling and modelling.

Application-centric Tactics. Application-centric tactics leverage knowledge on these decisions to reduce modelling and sampling efforts (**C,T**) maintaining accuracy (**A**).

T8 - Composition Type. In a composition, the configuration space rapidly increases with the number of functions. As an example, if we consider a simple sequence of three functions, the configuration space for the `memory` knob would be 10112^3 for AWS Lambda. However, making assumptions on the type of composition allows reducing the configuration space. In the context of the example, a function chain [4], enables observing each function in isolation, followed by a suitable aggregation. Precisely, the sum of the individual functions' execution latencies becomes an estimate of the composition's latency, thus reducing cost (**C**) and time (**T**). This tactic finds implicit usage in [8] and [2].

T9 - Workload. It is possible to observe significantly different qualities for runs with different valid event inputs. Consequently, maintaining high accuracy requires observing a system under different workloads, therefore, increasing the number of runs. This tactic leverages knowledge on the impact of an event-inputs on system qualities to reduce the number of runs and benefit-cost (**C**) and time (**T**). Making wrong assumptions reduces the accuracy of configurations (**A**).

5   Conclusion

Serverless systems require configuration methods to deal with quality-sensitive configuration options. Results from a literature review indicate that industry and research propose isolated configuration methods that focus on accuracy but come with implicit assumptions on a system's architecture and unclear developers' time and cost investments. We synthesized the results into nine general tactics to aid developers in the design and evaluation of configuration methods. We do not claim completeness and invite fellow researchers to add more tactics. For future work, we propose a modular approach that allows easily combining different tactics to meet the requirements of a particular system context.

References

1. Agache, A., et al.: Firecracker: lightweight virtualization for serverless applications. In: 17th Symposium on Networked Systems Design and Implementation, NSDI '2020, USENIX Association, Feb 2020. https://doi.org/10.5555/3388242.3388273
2. Akhtar, N., et al.: Cose: configuring serverless functions using statistical learning. In: IEEE INFOCOM 2020 (2020). https://doi.org/10.1109/INFOCOM41043.2020.9155363
3. Ali, A., et al.: Batch: Machine learning inference serving on serverless platforms with adaptive batching. In: Proceedings of SC 2020. SC 2020, IEEE Press (2020)
4. Baldini, I., et al.: The serverless trilemma: function composition for serverless computing. In: Proceedings of ACM SIGPLAN 2017, Onward! 2017, ACM (2017). https://doi.org/10.1145/3133850.3133855
5. Christoforou, A., Andreou, A.S.: An effective resource management approach in a FaaS environment. In: ESSCA 2018, ESSCA 2018, vol. 2330 (2018)
6. Eismann, S., et al.: Predicting the costs of serverless workflows (2020). https://doi.org/10.1145/3358960.3379133

7. Eismann, S., et al.: Sizeless: predicting the optimal size of serverless functions (2021). https://arxiv.org/abs/2010.15162, preprint
8. Elgamal, T., et al.: Costless: optimizing cost of serverless computing through function fusion and placement. In: SEC. SEC'2018, IEEE, October 2018. https://doi.org/10.1109/SEC.2018.00029
9. Jonas, E., et al.: Cloud programming simplified: a berkeley view on serverless computing, February 2019. http://arxiv.org/abs/1812.03651
10. Joyner, S., et al.: Ripple: a practical declarative programming framework for serverless compute (2020). https://arxiv.org/abs/2001.00222
11. Kaviani, N., et al.: Towards serverless as commodity: a case of knative. In: Proceedings of 5th WOSC 2019, ACM (2019). https://doi.org/10.1145/3366623.3368135
12. Kitchenham, B.A.: Guidelines for performing systematic literature reviews in software engineering. Technical Report (2007)
13. Kuhlenkamp, J., Werner, S.: Benchmarking FaaS platforms: call for community participation. In: Proceedings of 4th WoSC 2018, ACM, December 2018. https://doi.org/10.1109/UCC-Companion.2018.00055
14. Kuhlenkamp, J., et al.: An evaluation of FaaS platforms as a foundation for serverless big data processing. In: Proceedings of UCC 2019, ACM (2019). https://doi.org/10.1145/3344341.3368796
15. Kuhlenkamp, J., et al.: All but one: FaaS platform elasticity revisited. SIGAPP Appl. Comput. Rev. **20**(3), 5–19 (2020). https://doi.org/10.1145/3429204.3429205
16. Kuhlenkamp, J., et al.: The ifs and buts of less is more: A serverless computing reality check. In: Proceedings of IC2E 2020, IEEE (2020)
17. Leitner, P., et al.: A mixed-method empirical study of function-as-a-service software development in industrial practice. J. Syst. Softw. **149** (2018). https://doi.org/10.1016/j.jss.2018.12.013
18. Saha, A., Jindal, S.: Emars: efficient management and allocation of resources in serverless. In: Proceedings of 11th CLOUD 2018, July 2018. https://doi.org/10.1109/CLOUD.2018.00113
19. Sánchez-Artigas, M., et al.: Primula: a practical shuffle/sort operator for serverless computing. In: Proceedings of 21st Middleware 2020, pp. 31–37. Middleware 2020, ACM (2020). https://doi.org/10.1145/3429357.3430522
20. Scheuner, J., Leitner, P.: Function-as-a-service performance evaluation: a multivocal literature review. Syst. Softw. (2020). https://doi.org/10.1016/j.jss.2020.110708
21. Schuler, L., et al.: Ai-based resource allocation: reinforcement learning for adaptive auto-scaling in serverless environments (2020). https://arxiv.org/abs/2005.14410, preprint
22. Sedefouglu, Ö., Sözer, H.: Cost minimization for deploying serverless functions. In: Proceedings of 36th SAC 2021, ACM (2021). https://doi.org/10.1145/3412841.3442069
23. Taibi, D., et al.: Patterns for serverless functions (function-as-a-service): A multivocal literature review. In: Proceedings of 10th CLOSER 2020, INSTICC, SciTePress (2020). https://doi.org/10.5220/0009578501810192
24. Tariq, A., et al.: Sequoia: enabling quality-of-service in serverless computing. In: Proceedings of 11th SoCC 2020, ACM (2020). https://doi.org/10.1145/3419111.3421306
25. Werner, S., Tai, S.: Application-platform co-design for serverless data processing. In: Proceedings of 19th ICSOC 2021 (2021). https://doi.org/10.1007/978-3-030-91431-8_39

The ArchIBALD Data Integration Platform: Bridging Fragmented Processes in the Building Industry

Nico Lässig[1(✉)], Melanie Herschel[1(✉)], Alexander Reichle[2], Carsten Ellwein[2], and Alexander Verl[2]

[1] IPVS - University of Stuttgart, Stuttgart, Germany
{nico.laessig,melanie.herschel}@ipvs.uni-stuttgart.de
[2] ISW - University of Stuttgart, Stuttgart, Germany
{alexander.reichle,carsten.ellwein,alexander.verl}@isw.uni-stuttgart.de

Abstract. While recent efforts in establishing digital technologies in the building industry model individual phases of the building process, the data involved in these phases largely remain in data silos. This prevents the global consideration of data across phases, e.g., to analyze these data to steer or adapt processes or guide decisions. The ArchIBALD information system architecture tackles this challenge. The architecture design allows bi-directional exchange of information (e.g., in the form of feedback-loops) across components to allow novel adaptive building processes based on data integration. This novel feature is used by methods to enrich available data with information necessary to match designed components to resources available to fabricate, transport, or otherwise handle these automatically. We showcase how ArchIBALD allows joint analysis of traditionally fragmented data on the use case of optimizing task assignment.

Keywords: Building industry · Data integration · Task mapping · Feedback-driven

1 Introduction

Architecture is of central ecological, economic, social, and cultural relevance. It profoundly impacts the life of humans who spend 87% of their lives in buildings and the demand for living space is predicted to nearly double within the next 30 years [8]. Furthermore, the building industry consumes more than 40% of global resources and energy today [6,8]. Through years of experience, the stages of a building process pipeline have been fairly optimized in a mainly manual way. However, it has proven to be very difficult to keep on track in bigger projects (e.g. by the Berlin airport [7]). In the world of digitization, we want to use such digital technologies to further support the projects and automize several

Supported by the Deutsche Forschungsgemeinschaft (DFG, German Research Foundation) under Germany's Excellence Strategy - EXC 2120/1 - 390831618.

J. De Weerdt and A. Polyvyanyy (Eds.): CAiSE Forum 2022, LNBIP 452, pp. 45–54, 2022.
https://doi.org/10.1007/978-3-031-07481-3_6

processes, e.g. in order to reduce environmental impact and delays of projects. While there have been initial efforts in terms of digitization in the building industry, it is still lagging behind (e.g., ranked second to last industry in terms of digitalization [3]).

Although digital technologies become increasingly available, their adoption is rather slow and typically only focused on isolated aspects of the building process due to the fragmented nature of the building industry. In the following, we will describe a typical building process pipeline, exemplified for constructing fibre-based structures like the Maison Fibre[1]. First, architects *design* the building. Therefore, they use software for computer-aided design (CAD) that lets them try out different designs, shapes, and sizes, e.g., of both the full fibre-based structure as well as individual panels. Once the design is completed, *engineering* takes over the process to determine how to realize the design, e.g., by running simulations for structural analysis to determine the compression and stress on different building components to identify a stable configuration to be built. Afterwards, components can be *manufactured*. This can be partly automated using computer-aided manufacturing (CAM), e.g., by translating the engineering specifications to machine settings for, e.g., fibre-winding robots involved in the manufacturing process. In the final step, computer-aided *construction* helps manage on-site resources (e.g., positioning cranes, containers) or supports accurately assembling the structure on the construction site, e.g., by guiding crane operations.

In each phase, data are produced and used. However, the data typically remain confined to one phase and are only rarely used across the different phases beyond a "handover" of selected data. The ArchIBALD information system architecture we present in this paper addresses this shortcoming. It is tailored to the building industry and integrates data produced along the process, with the goal of leveraging these combined data to feed back data-derived insights to individual phases. Such feedback can for instance serve to optimize selected processes, e.g., to improve productivity. For example, we may adapt fabrication due to deviations from the original design and project plan recognized on monitoring data from the construction site. We make the following contributions. (i) We introduce an **information system architecture** named ArchIBALD (Sect. 2). A novelty is the integration of explicit feedback channels that break the usual one-way-street of data processing pipelines. Our implementation of ArchIBALD includes several domain-specific components, including (ii) **data enrichment algorithms and tools** that leverage the novel feedback channels. These are needed because we observed that, in practice, some of the data we identified as relevant to bridge the CAD-CAM chain is either omitted by the data producers, or the used software does not provide or export the relevant data. (iii) To integrate the enriched data, we incorporate a **data matching algorithm** that automatically matches available machines and tools (e.g., cutting machine equipped with a saw) to tasks (e.g., cutting) that relate to specific design components (e.g., a door of a specific size) (Sect. 4). (iv) The integrated data form the basis

---

[1] Maison Fibre - International Architecture Exhibition - La Biennale di Venezia 2021, Italy.

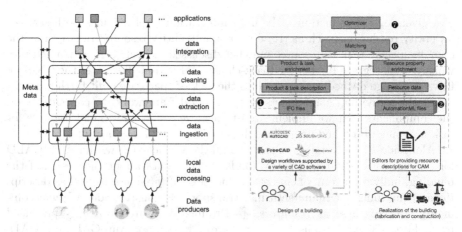

Fig. 1. General architecture of ArchIBALD   **Fig. 2.** Data processing for a use case

for a **use-case on optimized task assignment and scheduling** minimizing completion time (Sect. 5). We discuss related work alongside our contributions.

2 Data Integration and Analysis with ArchIBALD

This section describes the ArchIBALD architecture we devised as a digital data backbone for the next generation building process, which is the research focus of a larger research consortium we participate in[2].

One purpose of the data backbone is to allow the optimization or adaptation of processes in one phase, based on feedback from other phases, as illustrated in the introduction. Complementary approaches to ArchIBALD are being explored to advance the digitalization of the building industry. COMPAS [16] is a collaboration framework for the building industry. Its core focuses on the CAD phase, but extension packages are available for other phases. Nevertheless, the focus lies on CAD workflows rather than data flows. Speckle [2] is a data platform for architecture, engineering and construction (AEC). However, it so far focuses on data translation and exchange. ArchIBALD is the first architecture for end-to-end data integration and analysis in AEC that combines data lake principles [13, 17] with added-value services of limited scope (mediator-wrapper principle [14]) that allow multi-directional dataflow. Our design choices are founded on a requirement analysis conducted among 31 expert participants from the diverse and fragmented industries.

Figure 1 provides an overview of the ArchIBALD architecture. Data lake components are within rounded rectangles. Rectangles associated to different levels of the data lake represent services implemented as part of this level. Each level includes multiple services offering different functionalities within the scope

---

[2] Cluster of Excellence IntCDC: https://www.intcdc.uni-stuttgart.de.

of a given level. For instance, the data integration level includes both services for entity resolution (such as [15] for streaming entity resolution) as well as the domain-specific task-to-resource matcher discussed in Sect. 4. As explained previously, we integrate further feedback-channels. Figure 1 illustrates the feedback flows as orange dashed arrows. Due to the lack of space, we omit further details about the individual components of the general framework, to concentrate on the components that we implemented to achieve a first end-to-end use case for task mapping and scheduling. (i.e., the blue-shaded services in Fig. 1).

Alongside Fig. 2, we discuss the general data processing within ArchIBALD for our use case that requires two kinds of data: data about the design of the building, individual components etc., which we call *products*, as well as descriptions of machines for manufacturing, transport, or construction. We will commonly refer to these as *resources*. ❶ Product data are commonly produced by architects using various CAD software, e.g., Rhino, AutoCAD, FreeCAD, or SolidWorks. While these softwares have proprietary formats, they can commonly be translated to Industry Foundation Classes (IFC) [5]. Indeed, IFC is frequently used as open standard for exchanging data, especially about design and planning [5,12], in the context of Building Information Modeling (BIM) [4] that promises the digitalization across the phases of the building process. We thus consider IFC as the main format the data lake ingests for further processing. Similarly, ❷ tools allowing the editing of data conforming to the Automation Markup Language (AutomationML) [9] enable the description of resources and their capabilities. In the manufacturing industry, AutomationML is traditionally used during CAE and CAM to describe available machines and tools, or even entire facilities [9]. It can further be used to describe machinery and tools available during on-site construction, e.g., for transportation tasks. The data model of data ingested in ArchIBALD extends the data model we previously proposed [11] and given the limited space, is not discussed in further detail. ❸ During data extraction, we extract relevant information from IFC files, which includes product and task descriptions. Similarly, we also extract resource data from AutomationML files. The extracted data are summarized in Tables 1 and 2. In the real-world data we collected, we noted that, although the IFC data model comprises task descriptions, these are rarely present in ingested IFC files. Also, several relevant information about the geometry of products are often missing or not exported by the used software. To fill in the blanks, ❹/❺ enrichment services can be implemented to obtain the missing but relevant data as part of data cleaning. Section 3 summarizes the services we implemented that take advantage of the multi-directional data and message flow that our architecture supports. For data integration ❻, we devise a matching algorithm that associates products to resources, depending on the tasks associated to a product (Sect. 4). Feedback is provided in case that at least one task cannot be performed by any machine. Finally, the integrated data are used to ❼ optimize task assignment and scheduling.

Table 1. IFC extraction

Description	Parameter
Set of tasks	T
Implicit subtasks	$st \in t \ \forall t \in T$
Priority of a task	$prio_t \in \mathbb{N} \ \forall t \in T$
Set of products	P
Set of material categories	K
Set of concrete products	$P_{conc} \subseteq P : \forall p \in P_{conc} : k_p \in \{BreakBulk, PalletCargo\}$
Set of non-concrete products	$P_{nc} = P \backslash P_{conc}$
Set of products used in a task	$P_t \subseteq P \ \forall t \in T$
Material category	$k_p \in K \ \forall p \in P$
Product weight	$w_p \in \mathbb{R}_{>0} \ \forall p \in P$
Concrete product height	$height_p \in \mathbb{R}_{>0} \ \forall p \in P_{conc}$
Concrete product width	$width_p \in \mathbb{R}_{>0} \ \forall p \in P_{conc}$
Concrete product length	$length_p \in \mathbb{R}_{>0} \ \forall p \in P_{conc}$
Non-concrete product volume	$v_p \in \mathbb{R}_{>0} \ \forall p \in P_{nc}$
Previously finished tasks	$B_t \subset T \ \forall t \in T$

Table 2. AutomationML extraction

Description	Parameter
Set of machines	M
Set of skills	S
#available machines	$a_m \in \mathbb{N} \ \forall m \in M$
Cost (hourly) of the machine	$c_m \in \mathbb{R}_{>0} \ \forall m \in M$
Maximum allowed weight	$w_m \in \mathbb{R}_{>0} \ \forall m \in M$
Set of skills of a machine	$S_m \subseteq S \ \forall m \in M$
Maximum allowed height	$height_s \in \mathbb{R}_{>0} \ \forall s \in S_m$
Maximum allowed width	$width_s \in \mathbb{R}_{>0} \ \forall s \in S_m$
Maximum allowed length	$length_s \in \mathbb{R}_{>0} \ \forall s \in S_m$
Maximum available volume	$v_s \in \mathbb{R}_{>0} \ \forall s \in S_m$
Type of task handled via skill	$t_s \in T \ \forall s \in S$
Material category handled via skill	$k_s \in K \ \forall s \in S$
Set of attributes all attributes	A
Skill-related attributes	$A_s \subseteq A \ \forall s \in S$

3 Data Cleaning

During data cleaning, data quality characteristics relevant to higher-level applications are analyzed and, should the quality not be sufficient for the target applications, efforts are put into improving the quality. In ArchIBALD, data cleaning services consider the extracted data with respect to the target application. Leveraging the capability of ArchIBALD of multi-directional channels (as opposed to a classical sequential data processing pipeline), we implement several services to improve the quality, either by sending the corresponding feedback to the data providers or by applying automatic algorithms with feedback to or interaction with other services (see dashed orange arrows in Fig. 2). These address the following problems as described.

Despite IFC including classes to attach tasks to products, in practice, it is rarely done. The reason for this is that architects typically focus on the design of a building and are not concerned with its realization. Also, the IFC export facilities of the commonly used software often do not include exporting task information. Since the task information is crucial to automate the translation of a design to a production or construction plan and schedule, we devise a graphical tool that allows architects to easily add tasks to products. That is, the product and task enrichment service automatically determines if task information is missing and if so, sends a request to data producers to add the relevant data. The editor displays previously defined tasks and allows to add or edit task-specific IFC classes and attributes. The enrichment component further takes care of propagating the result of enrichment back to the IFC file.

We further noticed that information on the height, length, width, and volume of an object via property sets is frequently missing. In our application, this information is relevant to detect if a particular product can be handled by a particular resource. Thus, when the product and task enrichment service recognizes that these data are missing, it launches an automatic procedure to compute a bounding cuboid for the shape of an object (e.g., using existing algorithms [18]). The result is fed back to the IFC file, also triggering an update of the extracted data.

The resource property enrichment service works analogously to the task enrichment described above.

4   Data Integration

After data cleaning, the data are adequately prepared to be integrated. In this section, we present the matching service that matches tasks to resources based on the associated products. This amounts to solving a constraint satisfaction problem that checks, for each task t whether resources with the ability to execute the task are available. This matching is performed in three steps: First, we match individual tasks to machines. These individual tasks correspond to subtasks if $t \in T$ includes implicit subtasks, i.e., $st \in t$. Implicit subtasks can be defined if specific subtasks correlate, e.g., grip an object before cutting and then release the object again. Next, we derive task-to-resource matches, considering all combinations of possible resource assignments to subtasks. Finally, we prune based on domain-specific constraints.

Matching Individual Tasks to Resources. The first step checks each pair of subtask st of each task t and machine m and returns all matches where st can be performed with m. To simplify notation, if a task t comprises only one subtask, then $t = st$. More formally, $\forall t \in T : \forall st \in t, \forall m \in M$, we consider the following constraints:

- $\forall p \in P_t \; \exists s_i \in S_m : st \subseteq t_{s_i} \land k_p \subseteq k_{s_i}$: Checks if a subtask st can be handled by a resource or machine m, by checking that for all products p related to t, machine m has a skill s_i that can handle tasks of type st on the material k_p of product p;
- $\sum_{p \in p_t} w_p \leq w_m$: The maximum allowed weight w_m on the machine cannot be exceeded by the sum of weights of products;
- $p \in P_{conc} \rightarrow$ apply packing algorithm: Specific skills of some machines are restricted to be used on concrete products within specific size limitations. This could be due to the fact that, e.g., the robot arm of a static machine only has a specific frame to work within. We thus check if the respective skill of a machine for the current task can fit all products related to the task. This relies on packing algorithms, e.g., [10], to efficiently fill the frame machine;
- $p \in P_{nc} \rightarrow \sum_{p \in p_t} v_p \leq v_s$: Covers non-concrete products, checking the volume of the products against the maximum volume a machine can handle.

If all constraints are fulfilled for a pair of machine m and subtask st, the pair is flagged as a match. In this case, we additionally calculate an estimated duration of the subtask st via machine m, which is saved as $d_{m,st}$. For the lack of accurate predictions or real data on this (future work), our current implementation relies on randomized numbers generated in realistic ranges manually set for specific tasks.

Enumerating all Task-to-Resource Matches. As a task consists of multiple subtasks, the previous step can associate different machines to the subtasks of the (parent) task t, e.g., one machine per subtask. From this, we derive the task-to-resource matches as follows. With $\mathcal{M}_{st}$ being the set of resources matching a subtask st, $Comb = \Pi_{st_i \in t} \mathcal{M}_{st_i}$ denotes the cross product of all machine combinations possible to perform the subtasks of t. Then, our algorithm returns, $\forall comb_i \in Comb$, a match $(t, comb_i)$.

Match Pruning. Working with real-world use cases, we further encountered a special case for multi-step transport tasks consisting of the implicit subtasks take, transport and drop. Intuitively, if a machine transporting products cannot take or drop them, then the machine assigned for the take or drop task will have to do both, i.e., take and drop. For instance, if a transporter cannot actively take on products, another machine will have to actively take these objects and then drop them onto the transporter. In our implementation, we ensure that this kind of domain-specific constraint is considered and remove matches that do not satisfy it from the set of matches to be returned. Tasks containing gripping and releasing subtasks are handled similarly, since machines that grip an object also have to be the ones releasing them. The pruning can be extended to accommodate further rules, as the need may potentially arise in the future.

Should not all subtasks be matched, feedback is sent to data producers, e.g., to notify architects that a specific component of their design cannot be built as modeled by the tasks, or to notify the company on the construction site that a particular component may need special equipment.

5   Real Life Use Case

As mentioned in the introduction, the building industry suffers from stagnating productivity. Thus, we consider productivity optimization as a possible use case that benefits from the combined analysis of data from traditionally isolated phases of the building process, as described in the previous sections. This use case also "closes the feedback-loop" in the sense that its result can be further used to adapt local processes of the different stakeholders. The reported use case focuses on labor productivity, measured as completed work per fixed time-interval. Therefore, its objective function is the minimization of the overall duration of the execution of all tasks. We formalize the problem as an optimization problem taking additional domain-specific constraints into account, e.g., machines that are used in parallel are not allowed to exceed the availability amount limit or ensuring that pre-defined constraints on task orders and dependencies are satisfied. In general, finding an optimal task schedule is NP-hard [19] for a fixed assignment of tasks to machines. In our setting, we take multiple possible assignments into consideration, thus we devised a heuristic algorithm (details omitted due to space constraints and paper focus).

Our use case considers the "FZK Haus" [1]. This IFC4 file models the building of the research center in Karlsruhe. We added 12 necessary multi-step transportation tasks, consisting of the implicit subtasks take, transport, and drop. We also defined restrictions for possible task sequences. This use case bridges design and on-site construction, as we map products of the FZK Haus to resources available for transportation and construction on the building site. A set of resources is modeled in AutomationML, which includes tower cranes, an excavator, multiple wheelloaders and multiple transporters.

Using ArchIBALD, 10 out of the 12 tasks could be mapped to a set of machines. One of the tasks could not be mapped due to its material category, while a transport task of a prefabricate wall could not be mapped due to its size measurements. The constant feedback is very valuable to the data producers and to the project manager and planner. For instance, if available resources are not powerful enough to perform specific tasks during the construction, then the early feedback allows the project manager to adapt the overall approach by, for example, renting more powerful resources. This can help in reducing the amount of delays happening during the construction stage, due to the prevention of some unexpected issues arising during the construction phase itself.

Furthermore, the automated optimized task assignment and scheduling that builds on the integrated data shows close to optimal performance despite relying on a heuristic algorithm for performance reasons (e.g., average estimated time of 139 min instead of an optimal 128 min for multiple experimental settings). Overall, our preliminary evaluation based on the presented use case demonstrates the value of integrating data and the relevance of backchannels to components and stakeholders, incorporated into ArchIBALD.

6   Summary and Outlook

We presented ArchIBALD, a system architecture that aims at bridging the gap between existing data silos arising throughout fragmented processes in the building industry. We introduced its general architecture and data flow, which includes feedback channels and we described how to implement services in ArchIBALD to integrate IFC data from architectural design with AutomationML data from manufacturing or construction, when aiming to optimize task assignment and scheduling during off-site manufacturing or on-site construction. We applied ArchIBALD in a real-world use case and discussed the advantages of our automated feedback-driven approach. This is only a first step in our journey of providing data-informed services for improvements in the AEC industry, where we plan to devise further services within ArchIBALD and conduct a thorough evaluation in the future.

References

1. Institute for Automation and Applied Informatics (IAI): FZK Haus. Karlsruhe Institute of Technology (KIT) (2016). https://www.ifcwiki.org/index.php?title=KIT_IFC_Examples
2. Speckle, Aec Systems Ltd (2020). http://speckle.systems
3. Agarwal, R., Chandrasekaran, S., Sridhar, M.: Imagining Construction's Digital Future. McKinsey & Company, Atlanta (2016)
4. Azhar, S.: Building information modeling (BIM): trends, benefits, risks, and challenges for the AEC industry. Leadersh. Manage. Eng. **11**(3), 241–252 (2011)
5. Borrmann, A., Beetz, J., Koch, C., Liebich, T., Muhic, S.: Industry foundation classes: a standardized data model for the vendor-neutral exchange of digital building models. In: Borrmann, A., König, M., Koch, C., Beetz, J. (eds.) Building Information Modeling, pp. 81–126. Springer, Cham (2018). https://doi.org/10.1007/978-3-319-92862-3_5
6. Cao, X., Dai, X., Liu, J.: Building energy-consumption status worldwide and the state-of-the-art technologies for zero-energy buildings during the past decade. Energy Build. **128**, 198–213 (2016)
7. Connolly, K.: 'We were a laughing stock': Berlin airport finally finished as covid bites. The Guardian (2020)
8. Dean, B., Dulac, J., Petrichenko, K., Graham, P.: Towards zero-emission efficient and resilient buildings.: Global status report (2016)
9. Drath, R., Luder, A., Peschke, J., Hundt, L.: AutomationML-the glue for seamless automation engineering. In: IEEE International Conference on Emerging Technologies and Factory Automation, pp. 616–623 (2008)
10. Dube, E.L., Kanavathy, R., Woodview, P.: Optimizing three-dimensional bin packing through simulation. In: International Conference Modelling, Simulation, and Optimization (2006)
11. Ellwein, C., Reichle, A., Herschel, M., Verl, A.: Integrative data processing for cyber-physical off-site and on-site construction promoting co-design. Procedia CIRP **100**, 451–456 (2021)
12. European Construction Sector Observatory. Digitalisation in the construction sector (2021)
13. Fang, H.: Managing data lakes in big data era: what's a data lake and why has it became popular in data management ecosystem. In: IEEE International Conference on Cyber Technology in Automation, Control, and Intelligent Systems, pp. 820–824 (2015)
14. Garcia-Molina, H., et al.: The TSIMMIS approach to mediation: data models and languages. J. Intell. Inf. Syst. **8**(2), 117–132 (1997). https://doi.org/10.1023/A:1008683107812
15. Gazzarri, L., Herschel, M.: End-to-end task based parallelization for entity resolution on dynamic data. In: IEEE International Conference on Data Engineering, pp. 1248–1259 (2021)
16. Mele, T.V., Liew, A., Echenagucia, T.M., Rippmann, M., et al.: Compas: a framework for computational research in architecture and structures (2017). http://compas-dev.github.io/compas/
17. Nargesian, F., Zhu, E., Miller, R.J., Pu, K.Q., Arocena, P.C.: Data lake management: challenges and opportunities. Proc. VLDB Endowment **12**(12), 1986–1989 (2019)

18. O'Rourke, J.: Finding minimal enclosing boxes. Int. J. Comput. Inf. Sci. **14**(3), 183–199 (1985)
19. Ullman, J.D.: Np-complete scheduling problems. J. Comput. Syst. Sci. **10**(3), 384–393 (1975)

A Meta Survey of Quality Evaluation Criteria in Explanation Methods

Helena Löfström[1,3]([✉]) [ID], Karl Hammar[2], and Ulf Johansson[2]

[1] Department of Information Technology, University of Borås, Borås, Sweden
[2] Department of Computing, Jönköping University, Jönköping, Sweden
[3] Jönköping International Business School, Jönköping, Sweden
{helena.lofstrom,karl.hammar,ulf.johansson}@ju.se

Abstract. The evaluation of explanation methods has become a significant issue in explainable artificial intelligence (XAI) due to the recent surge of opaque AI models in decision support systems (DSS). Explanations are essential for bias detection and control of uncertainty since most accurate AI models are opaque with low transparency and comprehensibility. There are numerous criteria to choose from when evaluating explanation method quality. However, since existing criteria focus on evaluating single explanation methods, it is not obvious how to compare the quality of different methods.

In this paper, we have conducted a semi-systematic meta-survey over fifteen literature surveys covering the evaluation of explainability to identify existing criteria usable for comparative evaluations of explanation methods.

The main contribution in the paper is the suggestion to use appropriate trust as a criterion to measure the outcome of the subjective evaluation criteria and consequently make comparative evaluations possible. We also present a model of explanation quality aspects. In the model, criteria with similar definitions are grouped and related to three identified aspects of quality; model, explanation, and user. We also notice four commonly accepted criteria (groups) in the literature, covering all aspects of explanation quality: Performance, appropriate trust, explanation satisfaction, and fidelity. We suggest the model be used as a chart for comparative evaluations to create more generalisable research in explanation quality.

Keywords: Explanation method · Evaluation metric · Explainable artificial intelligence · Evaluation of explainability · Comparative evaluations

1 Introduction

AI model-based *Decision support systems* (DSS) have become increasingly popular due to their possibility of solving a variety of tasks, such as music recommendations or medical diagnosis. However, the highly accurate AI models lack

This research is partly founded by the Swedish Knowledge Foundation through the Industrial Research School INSiDR.

J. De Weerdt and A. Polyvyanyy (Eds.): CAiSE Forum 2022, LNBIP 452, pp. 55–63, 2022.
https://doi.org/10.1007/978-3-031-07481-3_7

both transparency and comprehensibility in their predictions, which has caused a new field to emerge; *explainable artificial intelligence* (XAI). In this field, the goal is to explain the opaque AI models with the help of explanation methods. However, the interest in explainability has simultaneously led to confusion on numerous fronts; it is, e.g., not clear how to evaluate and compare the quality of explanation methods [1].

The goal of explanations is to strengthen the user in making high-quality decisions by identifying when to trust and not trust the predictions, i.e., to make the user trust the system appropriately. However, many studies that evaluate explanation methods focus on how users experience explanations rather than the degree to which those explanations guide good decision-making. Furthermore, there are no generally accepted criteria for comparative evaluations. Instead, it is up to the individual researcher to decide which criterion to use. At the same time, there are many criteria to choose among, which makes it challenging to compare results from different evaluations. The main research objective in this study was to investigate if there exist generally accepted evaluation criteria, with a well-established method, that is possible to use for comparative evaluations of explanation methods.

A semi-systematic meta-survey was applied to fulfil the research objective. To ensure the quality of our research and find all related papers, we followed the methodology according to [2] but also took into consideration [3]. The study included fifteen literature surveys, covering a theoretical maximum of more than 2700 research articles. The methodology in the paper is divided into three steps: *Designing* the review (including choice of search terms, databases, inclusion and exclusion criteria, which type of information to extract, and the type of analysis), *conducting the review* with documentation of the process, and *analysing* the results based on the choices made in the design. The literature was collected from the areas of *Computer Science, Social Science, Business and Marketing Science* as well as *Decision Science* and limited to evaluation criteria for explanation methods. When the final sample was selected, the surveys were analysed to find evaluation criteria (definitions, usage, and quality threshold value). Each evaluation criterion was initially documented separately and then grouped based on definition and aspect of explanation quality. For a detailed description of the methodology in the study, see [4]. Several criteria were subjective and lacked method, which caused challenges in comparing the definitions.

The contributions of this paper are:

- We suggest measuring the outcome of the subjective evaluation criteria and thus make comparative evaluations possible.
- We also present a model, identifying existing evaluation criteria from four different research areas, the aspect of quality they measure and how they relate to each other.

The remainder of this paper is structured as follows: the next section provides a summary of the concept of post hoc explanation methods, while the results and discussion are presented in Sect. 3. The paper ends with some concluding remarks in Sect. 4.

2   Post Hoc Explanations

Research in explanations can be divided into two main focus areas [5,6]; transparency through interpretable models (interpretability) and *post-hoc* explanation methods for explaining opaque models (explainability). Post-hoc explanation methods apply to the output of the underlying model and create a simplified and interpretable model based on the relation between feature values and the prediction (see Fig. 1).

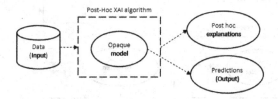

Fig. 1. The extraction of Post-hoc explanations, inspired by [7]

The relationships in the interpretable model are presented as explanations and can be, e.g., pixels in pictures, feature importance charts or words in texts, highlighting which features (pixels or words) that are important for the prediction. Explanations are intended to explain the model's strengths and weaknesses to the users, creating a possibility to identify erroneous predictions and an understanding of the model's rationale.

3   Results and Discussion

Evaluations of the use of explanation methods could be divided into three aspects of quality; *model, explanation,* and *user* (see Fig. 2) [1,8–11]. In line with earlier research, we found that many evaluation criteria had various names in different studies. Based on the findings in the literature, we grouped the criteria on how they were defined: how the criteria were *collected*, if the criteria were *objective* (system output) or *subjective* (human thoughts/output), and what the criteria were supposed to *measure*. We used the most common or well-established names in the surveys as the name of the criteria (groups). After the analysis, we identified eleven criteria.

3.1   The User Aspect

The majority of the criteria in the user aspect are subjective and challenging to measure. However, since changes in the subjective criteria cause the user's *mental model* to change during the usage of the system, we consider the mental model as a container of these criteria and not a criterion of its own [7,10,12–14]. The resulting four criteria connected to the user aspect were:

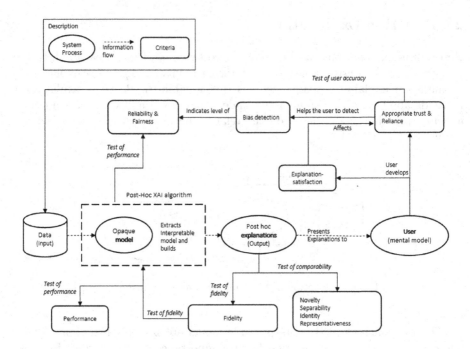

Fig. 2. High-level model of the criteria groups in the different aspects of explanation quality.

- **Trust**: a highly used criterion and referred to in [14] as one of the absolute most important criteria for success. However, it is inherently subjective and therefore challenging to measure [8,11,14–16]. The definition of trust has been discussed in multiple research disciplines including psychology [17] and machine learning [11]. In [18] trust is related to both credibility and an attitude that an agent will help achieve an individual's goals in a situation characterised by uncertainty and vulnerability. Trust has, in that way, two aspects: i) the user's willingness to act based on the recommendation of the system and ii) their confidence in the correctness of the prediction [19]. In earlier research [17,20] two extreme reactions have been studied when users doubt the correctness of a system's predictions; they put the system aside, not trusting it (*disuse*), or they set their doubts aside and blindly trust the system (*misuse*). There is, in other words, problematic to merely try to increase user's trust in the system. There must be some form of alignment between the perceived and actual performance of the system.
- **Appropriate trust**: trust is also possible to define as an attitude formed by information about the system and previous experiences. The attitude creates intentions whether or not to rely on, or trust, the system resulting in *reliance* [14,21]. Under this definition, trust is directly connected to the quality of explanations, in the form of *appropriate trust* or *calibrated trust* [7,8,10,11,13–15,22–27]. A good mental model is a requirement for develop-

ing appropriate trust [15]. The criterion is one of the outcomes of the user's mental model (see Fig. 2), consisting of the user aspect (human trust in the system) and the explanation aspect (the output of the system) [8,22]. When identifying the level of appropriate trust, the users try to identify the correct and erroneous predictions. The ideal result is a 1:1 situation where all correct and erroneous predictions are identified (see figure 3). All other cases lead to either *misuse* (overuse) or *disuse* (under-use). Appropriate trust could, in other words, be defined as the user's accuracy; to what degree the users act according to the data.

- Appropriate trust is also closely connected to **bias detection** which is one of the desired outcomes of explanations. Bias is possible to detect when the user has high appropriate trust and, in that way, can identify the general patterns of errors in the system [14,24,26,27]. However, [24] defines the term as more of a data set desiderata. The criterion could be seen as the joint outcome of the user's mental model, together with appropriate trust, creating reliance (see Fig. 2).

- **Explanation satisfaction**: to what extent an explanation user interface or an explanation is suitable for the intended purpose [28]. This criterion is the outcome of the mental model (see Fig. 2). The evaluation is conducted with Likert scales, with questions similar to, e.g., if the user understands the explanations and finds them relevant.

	Prediction	
	T:T	T:F
Actual value	F:T	F:F

Fig. 3. Appropriate trust is the user's ability to detect (trust) the true predictions and detect (distrust) the false predictions.

3.2   The Explanation Aspect

The *Explanation* aspect of quality is placed between the model aspect and the user aspect, focusing on the evaluations of the explanations. It is sometimes referred to as the *user-machine performance*, highlighting the relation between the machine and the human. The criteria are objective but can include humans in the evaluation. Five criteria were identified in this aspect:

- **Fidelity**: reflects how accurately the explanation method mirrors the underlying model [6,7,10–12,24–26]. The fidelity could also be used to measure the difference between description accuracy given by the system and the description accuracy assessed by the user, including a more subjective perspective [24].

- **Identity, Separability, Novelty, and Representativeness**: in [11] the authors suggests several new metrics for evaluation of explanations. The criteria are related to fidelity and catch the explanations' correctness, although they can be calculated without the inclusion of humans. The three first criteria compare the explanations between different instances; i) identical instances should have identical explanations, ii) non-identical instances should not have identical explanations, and iii) the instance should not come from a region in instance space far from the training data. Finally, representativeness measures how many instances are covered by the explanation.

3.3 The Model Aspect

In the explanation aspect, the output from the user aspect, or mental model, is fed back to the system via the criteria, *appropriate trust* and *reliance* (see Fig. 2). Several evaluation criteria are connected to the underlying model's aspect of quality:

- **Performance**: a group of criteria that, together with appropriate trust, is most often referred to in the surveys as important to the quality of the explanations. The criteria indicates the level of correctness of the model against the actual target, such as *accuracy* and is measured similar to appropriate trust (see Fig. 3) [1, 7, 10, 11, 13, 14, 16, 23–26, 29].
- **Fairness**: the opposite to bias, i.e., to what degree does the model have general errors patterns. However, they measure the same aspect of quality. A model without bias is unbiased [8], i.e., have a high level of fairness. The level of bias indicates the level of fairness and also the level of reliability of the model (see Fig. 2). The criteria are considered by some authors more of desiderata and are therefore somewhat lacking in method description [11].
- **Reliability**: close to the criterion Accuracy, since it signals a confidence measure of the model to the user in a specific situation [7, 8, 10, 11, 23, 24]. Reliability is possible to measure in different ways. In, e.g., [10] the authors use questionnaires with likert scales and questions similar to if the XAI system is reliable.

3.4 Discussion

Comparative evaluations of explanation methods are challenging, and a general computational benchmark across all possible explanation methods is seen in [16] as unlikely to be possible due to the subjective characteristics. However, it is generally accepted that the mental model affects the level of appropriate trust and reliance in the system. If considering the mental model as a container of the subjective criteria, the outcome of the mental model would be possible to measure through the criteria appropriate trust (see, e.g., [10]). Although appropriate trust does not explicitly answer how the user experiences the explanations, it demonstrates if they fulfil one of the most crucial goals of explanation methods; if the user can detect correct and erroneous predictions. By measuring the outcome of the mental model through appropriate trust, we get an objective metric for the quality of the user aspect and create possibilities for comparative evaluations of explanation methods.

It is essential to highlight that we do not consider the subjective criteria unnecessary or unimportant to measure. In contrast, we acknowledge them as crucial for quality. When evaluating a single explanation method, it could be vital to follow subjective criteria changes. However, if the evaluation intends to gain comparable results, we recommend using the appropriate trust criteria.

4   Conclusion

This paper conducted a semi-systematic meta-survey over fifteen surveys to find commonly accepted evaluation criteria, with a well-defined method possible to use in comparative evaluations. The field was found to focus on human-in-the-loop evaluations, creating severe challenges for quality comparisons.

The major contribution of the paper is the suggestion of using the criterion *appropriate trust* as an outcome metric of the subjective criteria in the mental model, overcoming the problems with comparative evaluations. We also present a high-level model of explanation method quality, identifying three aspects of quality: *model, explanation,* and *user*. The quality of an explanation method is suggested to be a composition of all three aspects. We also identified ten evaluation criteria (groups) in different quality aspects and their relation in the meta-survey. Four of the criteria were mentioned in more than half of the surveys as necessary for the quality of an explanation method: *performance, appropriate trust, explanation satisfaction,* and *fidelity*. These criteria cover all three aspects of explanation quality, and we suggest that they are used when researchers want to make their evaluations comparable.

The mental model consists of several subjective criteria, all of which can affect the output. We suggest as future work evaluations with human respondents studying how the subjective criteria affect the level of appropriate trust in the system.

References

1. Murdoch, W.J., Singh, C., Kumbier, K., Abbasi-Asl, R., Yu, B.: Definitions, methods, and applications in interpretable machine learning. Proc. Natl. Acad. Sci. **116**(44), 22071–22080 (2019)
2. Snyder, H.: Literature review as a research methodology: an overview and guidelines. J. Bus. Res. **104**, 333–339 (2019)
3. Webster, J., Watson, R.T.: Analyzing the past to prepare for the future: writing a literature review. MIS Q. xiii–xxiii (2002)
4. Löfström, H., Hammar, K., Johansson, U.: A meta survey of quality evaluation criteria in explanation methods (2022)

5. Lundberg, S.M., Lee, S.I.: A unified approach to interpreting model predictions. In: Proceedings of the 31st International Conference on Neural Information Processing Systems, pp. 4768–4777 (2017)
6. Moradi, M., Samwald, M.: Post-hoc explanation of black-box classifiers using confident itemsets. Expert Syst. Appl. **165**, 113941 (2021)
7. Arrieta, A.B., et al.: Explainable artificial intelligence (XAI): Concepts, taxonomies, opportunities and challenges toward responsible AI. Inf. Fusion **58**, 82–115 (2020)
8. Doshi-Velez, F., Kim, B.: Towards a rigorous science of interpretable machine learning. arXiv preprint arXiv:1702.08608 (2017)
9. Gilpin, L.H., Bau, D., Yuan, B.Z., Bajwa, A., Specter, M., Kagal, L.: Explaining explanations: an overview of interpretability of machine learning. In: 2018 IEEE 5th International Conference on Data Science and Advanced Analytics (DSAA), pp. 80–89. IEEE (2018)
10. Hoffman, R.R., Mueller, S.T., Klein, G., Litman, J.: Metrics for explainable AI: challenges and prospects. arXiv preprint arXiv:1812.04608 (2018)
11. Carvalho, D.V., Pereira, E.M., Cardoso, J.S.: Machine learning interpretability: a survey on methods and metrics. Electronics **8**, 832 (2019)
12. Mueller, S.T., Hoffman, R.R., Clancey, W., Emrey, A., Klein, G.: Explanation in human-AI systems: a literature meta-review, synopsis of key ideas and publications, and bibliography for explainable AI. arXiv preprint arXiv:1902.01876 (2019)
13. Mohseni, S., Zarei, N., Ragan, E.D.: A multidisciplinary survey and framework for design and evaluation of explainable AI systems. arXiv, pp. arXiv-1811 (2018)
14. Gunning, D., Aha, D.W.: Darpa's explainable artificial intelligence program. AI Mag **40**(2), 44–58 (2019)
15. Hoff, K.A., Bashir, M.: Trust in automation: integrating empirical evidence on factors that influence trust. Hum. Factors **57**(3), 407–434 (2015)
16. Zhou, J., Gandomi, A.H., Chen, F., Holzinger, A.: Evaluating the quality of machine learning explanations: a survey on methods and metrics. Electronics **10**(5), 593 (2021)
17. Dzindolet, M.T., Peterson, S.A., Pomranky, R.A., Pierce, L.G., Beck, H.P.: The role of trust in automation reliance. Int. J. Hum Comput Stud. **58**(6), 697–718 (2003)
18. Pavlidis, M., Mouratidis, H., Islam, S., Kearney, P.: Dealing with trust and control: a meta-model for trustworthy information systems development. In: 2012 Sixth International Conference on Research Challenges in Information Science (RCIS), pp. 1–9. IEEE (2012)
19. Yang, F., Huang, Z., Scholtz, J., Arendt, D.L.: How do visual explanations foster end users' appropriate trust in machine learning? In: Proceedings of the 25th International Conference on Intelligent User Interfaces, pp. 189–201 (2020)
20. Marsh, S., Dibben, M.R.: Trust, untrust, distrust and mistrust – an exploration of the dark(er) side. In: Herrmann, P., Issarny, V., Shiu, S. (eds.) iTrust 2005. LNCS, vol. 3477, pp. 17–33. Springer, Heidelberg (2005). https://doi.org/10.1007/11429760_2
21. Ekman, F., Johansson, M., Sochor, J.: Creating appropriate trust in automated vehicle systems: a framework for HMI design. IEEE Trans. Hum. Mach. Syst. **48**(1), 95–101 (2017)
22. McDermott, P.L., Ten Brink, R.N.: Practical guidance for evaluating calibrated trust. In: Proceedings of the Human Factors and Ergonomics Society Annual Meeting, vol. 63, pp. 362–366. SAGE Publications Sage CA, Los Angeles (2019)

23. Chromik, M., Schuessler, M.: A taxonomy for human subject evaluation of black-box explanations in xai. In ExSS-ATEC@ IUI (2020)
24. Das, A., Rad, P.: Opportunities and challenges in explainable artificial intelligence (XAI): a survey. arXiv preprint arXiv:2006.11371 (2020)
25. Adadi, A., Berrada, M.: Peeking inside the black-box: a survey on explainable artificial intelligence (XAI). IEEE Access **6**, 52138–52160 (2018)
26. Wang, D., Yang, Q., Abdul, A., Lim, B.Y.: Designing theory-driven user-centric explainable AI. In: Proceedings of the 2019 CHI Conference on Human Factors in Computing Systems, CHI 2019, pp. 1–15, New York, Association for Computing Machinery (2019)
27. Zhang, Y., Chen, X.: Explainable recommendation: a survey and new perspectives. arXiv preprint arXiv:1804.11192 (2018)
28. Holzinger, A., Carrington, A., Müller, H.: Measuring the quality of explanations: the system causability scale (SCS). KI-Künstliche Intelligenz, pp. 1–6 (2020)
29. Linardatos, P., Papastefanopoulos, V., Kotsiantis, S.: Explainable AI: a review of machine learning interpretability methods. Entropy **23**(1), 18 (2021)

Designing a Self-service Analytics System for Transportation Supplier Selection

Sven Michalczyk[(✉)], Nicolas Breitling, and Alexander Maedche[(iD)]

Institute of Information Systems and Marketing (IISM), Karlsruhe Institute of Technology (KIT), Karlsruhe, Germany
{sven.michalczyk,alexander.maedche}@kit.edu

Abstract. Today, the selection of suppliers is expanded from a pure cost-oriented view to consider multiple criteria such as delivery time, quality, and risks. Buyers in the business analyst's role (BA) in global logistic departments are responsible for covering transportation demands. For supplier selection, they must allocate hundreds of items to an optimal set of suppliers. In interviews, we examined a high dependency on Data Scientists and Data Engineers. Currently, BAs achieve only non-optimal solutions because they lack the required knowledge and adequate tools to perform this analytical process independently. Against this backdrop, we present the design and evaluation of a self-service analytics (SSA) system that helps BAs to select suppliers for transportation demands considering multiple decision criteria. We formulate a linear optimization problem that BAs can parametrize and analyze with our SSA system. Our proposed SSA system enables BAs to improve the supplier selection process and showcases the potential of SSA systems to utilize optimization models.

Keywords: Supplier Selection Problem · Optimal Order Allocation · Self-Service Analytics · Linear Programming · Operations Research

1 Introduction

Supplier selection is becoming an increasingly complex decision-making problem in highly globalized supply chains. The buyer's choice is expanded from a purely cost-oriented view to include critical factors such as delivery time, quality, and risks [1]. Choosing the supplier with the lowest cost is not necessarily the best choice, as companies must distribute their demands among several suppliers to diversify risk. In research, this is known as the supplier selection problem. The objective is to allocate items among suppliers optimally [2]. In this regard, research suggested different linear programming approaches (LP), considering a single objective [3] or multi-objective [4], formalized as a non-integer, integer, or binary problem [5]. Although LP is an established approach, recent advances in computing power, algorithms, and data availability have made it possible to solve such problems more effectively and efficiently [6].

However, formulating the supplier selection problem as an LP model and applying solvers is a complex endeavor. Although research has focused on simplifying modeling

J. De Weerdt and A. Polyvyanyy (Eds.): CAiSE Forum 2022, LNBIP 452, pp. 64–72, 2022.
https://doi.org/10.1007/978-3-031-07481-3_8

languages, proficiency in mathematics and LP is still required [7]. According to interviews conducted by us and Schuff et al. [8], most buyers in the role of business analysts (BAs) do not have this knowledge. Recently, Self-Service Analytics (SSA) research started to investigate how BAs can be enabled to leverage analytics (e.g., machine learning, short ML) on their own [e.g., 9]. SSA systems are characterized by easy-to-use interfaces [10] and minimize the dependency on experts in analytics (i.e., Data Scientists, short DSs) and data preparation (i.e., Data Engineers, short DEs) [11].

Against this backdrop, an SSA system based on LP is a promising approach to enable BAs. We collaborated with the global logistic department of our industry partner to tackle the recurrent problem of selecting suppliers for an optimal allocation of transportation items. Thereby, we raise the following research question: *How to design an SSA system for BAs to apply LP models for selecting transportation suppliers?*

We conducted semi-structured interviews following the guidelines of Seaman [12] to elicit the underlying requirements. We developed an LP model for supplier selection. On this basis, we implemented and evaluated an SSA system that (1) facilitates the data preparation and (2) the application of the implemented LP model with an easy-to-use interface. To evaluate our system, we conducted think-aloud sessions with eight BAs [13]. In the remainder of this article, we describe the related work and supplier selection practices. Subsequently, we introduce the formalization of our LP approach and the user interface (UI), followed by an evaluation and a conclusion.

2 Supplier Selection Problem

Previous research investigated the supplier selection problem [2] and distinguished the classification of mathematical optimization for supplier selection in single-objective and multi-objective programming. Thereby, LP, a special case of integer programming (i.e., restriction of the decision variables in the feasible solution to integer variables), is the omnipresent approach used. Single-objective models consider one criterion as the objective function, while other criteria, such as quality and lead-time, are modeled as constraints. Multi-objective models consider multiple criteria as objective functions simultaneously [14]. In particular, Che and Wang [3] used LP to model supplier selection by considering order quantity allocation to minimize the utility function of order items. Talluri [5] developed a binary integer LP model to evaluate alternative supplier bids based on the target bids of buyers. Thereby, the optimal bids are evaluated based on demand and capacity constraints. Ruiz-Torres et al. [15] applied stochastic programming and shifted the focus from finding a cost-optimal solution to incorporating criteria such as risk and suppliers' qualitative and economic performance. In the context of multiple supply sources and separate demand points, they integrated a probability of failure to supply required quantities. Narasimhan et al. [4] constructed a multi-objective LP model to select suppliers simultaneously by determining an optimal order quantity. Thus, LP is an established approach and applicable to optimize the allocation of transportation items to a set of suppliers by using various constraints [2, 7]. Although research started to simplify modeling languages [7], LP still requires mathematical modeling knowledge that most BAs do not have [8]. Against this backdrop, BAs might use Excel Add-Ins for mathematical optimization [e.g., 16]. Those Add-Ins allow building large-scale optimization models without writing code in a spreadsheet environment. Although BAs are familiar with Excel, the Add-Ins still require LP expertise and are limited in the usability and the formulation of constraints.

3 Self-service Analytics System for Supplier Selection

3.1 Practices and Requirements of Transportation Supplier Selection

To determine the requirements of the SSA system, we investigated practices of transportation supplier selection (TSS) in **semi-structured interviews** [15] with five BAs. Our interview guideline contained five leading questions. First, we asked about the TSS criteria and potential constraints. Second, we asked to sketch the TSS process with pen and paper. Third, we were interested in which roles are involved in this process. Fourth, we asked about experiences in data engineering and LP. Fifth and last, we asked BAs about their requirements for an SSA system for TSS. In the analysis step, assisted by MAXQDA, we extracted TSS criteria and captured four key issues from BAs' practices. On this basis, we identified seven requirements for an SSA system.

At our industry partner, TSS refers to a process in which BAs must make a contract awarding decision on transportation demands. BAs are responsible for allocating approximately 100 Million Euros. BAs collect bids from suppliers on logistic services referred to as items. Changing suppliers, items, exchange rates, or regional prices make each TSS unique and a recurring task for BAs. In their awarding decision, BAs consider the following **TSS criteria**: costs, lead times, supply coverage, item bundling, prior experience such as delivery reliability, and lastly, strategic relevance like future partnerships. Furthermore, BAs mentioned several constraints (see Sect. 3.2.)

Interviews revealed that BAs currently rely on DSs and DEs. They create sheets (called ratecards) for suppliers to submit their bids for items. Subsequently, DEs prepare the data received from the suppliers, and DSs deploy dashboards for BAs to select suppliers. We identified **four key issues** in this process: (I) The data preparation is not automated because suppliers enter bids manually into ratecards which is prone to structural errors. (II) BAs could only analyze data in a descriptive dashboard without determining an optimal transportation item allocation to suppliers considering cost, quality, and performance. Hence, the current solution does not rely on LP. (III) DEs, and DSs are bottlenecks because they prepare the data manually and deploy dashboards. BA analysts stated that they must usually wait 2–3 days until DEs and DS are finished. The fourth interview question revealed that they could not do this independently because they lack the required data engineering expertise and knowledge in LP (IV). Hence, an SSA system has the potential to enable BAs while relieving DE and DS.

Finally, we asked BAs about their **requirements** for such a system. The first three requirements are related to the data engineering tasks making BAs independent from DEs (III). First, the system should provide functions for uploading data via drag and drop (requirement (a)). Next, the system should give recommendations to increase the data quality (b). The data quality check is necessary because BAs collect data from suppliers in which they enter their bids into ratecards manually. Potentially, data issues will occur (I). Furthermore, the system should merge data as input for the optimization (c). Because DSs are also critical bottlenecks (III), the system should allow the definition of an LP model code-free in business terminology of BAs (d). Thus, the system should provide an optimal solution to the TSS problem (II). In interviews, we gained the impression that BAs require an introduction to the system and an explanation of optimization results (IV), leading to (e): The system should provide explanations of LP. Lastly, BAs asked for export functionalities to be compatible with existing practices and tools (f), like the dashboards DSs deployed.

3.2 Linear Programming Model of the SSA System

We formalized constraints and the LP model based on the identified TSS criteria, addressing key issue II. First, the total costs (see (i) in Fig. 1) are represented by the sum of all individual costs per awarding decision that must be minimized. Second, each transportation item can be awarded to a supplier or left independent. To model this, overall selected suppliers (xii) and optimal awarded transportation items (xi) must become 1 or 0, respectively. We model this as binary decisions utilizing Boolean Variables [14]. Third, every transportation item is awarded to exactly one supplier (ii) if the supplier placed a bid (iii) and if BAs have nominated the supplier (iv). We have modeled this by relying on the established Big-M method [4, 14]. Fourth, if each supplier bet the least on one different transportation item, the mathematical optimum would select all possible suppliers with a marginal number of transportation items awarded, leading to a non-maintainable number of suppliers [14]. We followed the recommendations of Narasimhan et al. [4] and optimized for multiple objectives in single-objective LP by introducing constraints (ix) and (x). These constraints account for the number of items and, thus, the overall awarding volume by modeling the lower and upper boundaries of awarded transportation items. In doing so, we reduce both the complexity and the required computation time [2] because our data consists of a high number of items to allocate. Similarly, we introduced boundaries for the number of suppliers (v)–(vi) and item share (vii)–(viii). In this regard, we followed Narasimhan et al. [4], who modeled a threshold of the allocated volume to a supplier to account for the economics of its operations. Thus, we ensure that the awarded volume will satisfy the supplier, and a subsequent negotiation will probably lead to an agreement between both parties. Fifth, we model lead time as a constraint [4], because suppliers who offer the lowest price do not necessarily offer a lead time that meets expectations. (xiv). Sixth, a transportation lane regularly consists of thousands of transportation items from different origins to destinations. Thus, BA must identify bundling opportunities to maintain operational feasibility. In this regard, we define constraints to force the bundling of transportation items to suppliers with the following options: unidirectional origin to destination (xv), bidirectional origin to destination (xvi), or based on the dataset (xvii). Seventh and finally, some suppliers set higher or lower prices than the market average. They do this to get the contract, e.g., for strategic reasons, even though they cannot deliver the required quality. To counteract, we introduce a bonus respectively malus factor on the quotations (xiii). In this way, BAs can compensate for good performance, like delivery quality and reliability. At the same time, BAs can set a malus that penalizes suppliers for poor quality or consider the risk for unknown suppliers. In summary, we consider multiple criteria in the optimization (i.e., delivery time, uncertainty, quality, service level, risk management, sustainability). We relied on a single-criteria optimization to avoid an increase in modeling complexity

[14] and expected computation time, although multi-objective functions enable the identification of Pareto-optimal solutions [4]. We implemented the model in Python with the library ortools [17].

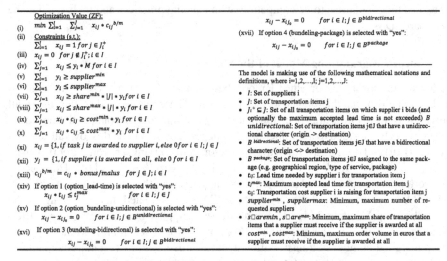

Fig. 1. LP model for transportation supplier selection

3.3 Implementation of the SSA System

In the following, we describe the implementation of collected requirements in an SSA system. The system guides BAs with five navigation tabs through the TSS (see Fig. 2). The first tab of the system, **Intro**, provides an onboarding in the form of textual explanations and visualizations. Additionally, we explain LP in simple terms and its value proposition, implementing requirement (e). In the next tab, **Ratecard Validation**, BAs can upload a ratecard collected from a supplier via drag-and-drop or file select (a). Subsequently, the system checks the uploaded data for errors. In an output box, the system automatically distinguishes between warnings and critical issues that require refinement, for instance, if bids are missing. In doing so, the system recommends actions to increase the data quality (b), which, for instance, BAs can forward to suppliers. After validating the ratecards, the system offers functionalities for **Upload, Process & Save Supplier Bidding Data** in the third tab. Implementing requirement (a), BAs can upload the data again via drag and drop (indicated by the red circle with (1) in Fig. 2.). Subsequently, the system checks for structural errors across ratecards (2). Once all ratecards are validated, BAs can define TSS criteria in business terminology (d), for instance, cost components (3) and a bonus or malus (4) to consider experiences or strategic partnerships with suppliers, without writing code (see Sect. 3.1). BAs get immediate feedback in the information box when they make a selection in the sidebar or an error occurs (5) (a) (d). We ensure that BAs do not require support from DE with the system's responses, accounting for (III). Finally, the system will merge the data as input for the optimization in a SQL database (6) (c). The fourth tab, **Power BI Dashboard Access**, accounts for the compatibility with existing practices (f). The system automatically creates the dashboards from the prepared data stored in the SQL database. BAs can access the dashboards through a library, which can also be used to retrieve previously created dashboards. BAs explicitly asked for these dashboards, although they do not offer an optimal solution (f). Hence, DSs will be relieved by the system, as DSs do not have to create the dashboards manually anymore (III).

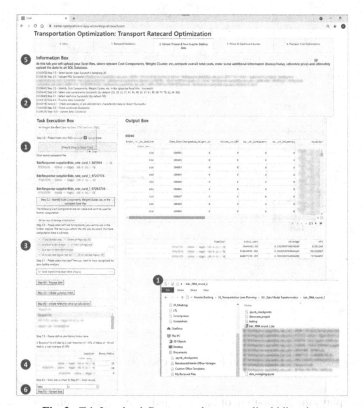

Fig. 2. Tab 2: upload, Process and save supplier biding data

The last tab, **Transport Cost Optimization,** is divided into three main areas, addressing (II). The sidebar on the left (7), named the task execution box, guides BAs through the parametrization of the model (the lower roman numbers refer to the implementation of the LP model's constraints; see Fig. 1). BAs can specify TSS criteria, set a time limit for the optimization (12), select suppliers for optimization (10), and define bundling options (11). To implement requirement (d), we used the business terminology of BAs, which can define the optimization without writing code. Furthermore, the system notifies BAs in case of faulty parameter combinations in tooltips attached to the input fields (e.g., 11) or after an optimization cycle (14) to ensure that only correct LP models are deployed (13). In doing so, we implement (e) and BAs' need for explanations (IV) (Fig. 3).

The output box at the right (8) shows the optimization' result. We selected the following visualizations to enhance data understanding and provide explanations (e): A

Fig. 3. Tab 4: Transport cost optimization

bar graph displays the distribution of the allocated volume per supplier in blue bars and the item share per supplier in red bars (15), addressing (III). Below, two tables break down the supplier allocation on the item code and country levels (16). Because BAs need detailed information for negotiations, we relied on tables. In doing so, the system provides information on different aggregation levels by using bar plots and tables. To ensure compatibility with existing practices (f), we integrate buttons to export the shown tables. The system recommends improvements after an optimization cycle (17), such as parameter changes (e). Finally, the storage box (9) shows a history of past optimizations.

4   Evaluation

We conducted think-aloud sessions with eight BAs (PE1–8). First, we introduced the functionalities of the tool. In the subsequent 45 min, we asked BAs to use our system to identify an optimal set of suppliers. Adhering to Nielsen [13], we prompt BAs to continuously verbalize their thoughts while using the system. We provided ratecards that suppliers' bids, characterized by costs, lead times, and coverage. The ratecards are the only input required in conjunction with the BAs' business expertise. Hence, relying on this real-world scenario, BAs must upload, validate, prepare, and analyze ratecards.

First, PE1 and PE4 considered the general explanations of the tool in **tab 0**. helpful to get an overview of the system. In **tab 1.**, all BAs agree that the measures to validate the data quality are essential because suppliers often make mistakes entering bids in the ratecards. PE1 highlights the data preparation function in **tab 2.** (3) *"there is no dependency as such on our own"*. In this regard, PE4 liked the feedback the system provides (5, 2): *"then I'm more confident, and I move to the next step"*. PE2 and PE3 liked that the SSA includes existing dashboards in **tab 3**. PE2 uses the dashboards to analyze ratecards in detail, giving suppliers feedback in an early phase of the TSS.

Almost all of the BAs were able to set up an LP model in **tab 4.**, even though they had no previous LP knowledge. PE2 concluded that *"[...] I don't need to have that much detailed analytical knowledge. [...] if it does not involve coding, then it is automatically an easy tool to refer to"*. The statement indicates that the sidebar structure (7) guides BAs skillfully through parameterization. PE4 stated that there are too many *"things to do [and] to select [while] not having the whole information. It put me on guessing what to select"*. PE3 did not understand the optimization time limit slider (12) and was insecure about continuing, requesting a detailed explanation of the parameters. The visualizations (8) helped BAs make sense of the model's output. In particular, PE2 concluded that *"now I know which country to which destination I will use for [supplier X] and which I want to use [supplier Y] as an optimal solution"*. One exception was the bar graph (13), where PE5 assumed having done something wrong due to the red color scheme. In turn, all BAs quickly understood the data in tables as they are familiar with tables from their daily work with Excel. Noteworthy, almost all BAs used the recommendations to generate further optimization results in the extensibility box (17) multiple times. PE2 stated that *"it says some recommendations for [...]. Start optimization again. Let us check. Oh, yes. I have a better combination"*. They naturally followed the recommendations by updating the parameters in the sidebar. The explanations in the form of tooltips in input fields facilitated their understanding of the LP model. Furthermore, PE5 liked *"the opportunity [...] to download it in Excel"*. All BAs agree as they can validate and communicate the results using a familiar tool like Excel.

In summary, PE1 mentioned that *"we restrict the time of analysis [...] the same time can be used for the core tasks [of negotiating]"*. PE6 agreed and said *"without having to ask someone or have to use something which is, you know, a frozen standard"*. Thus, the system resolves the dependencies of BAs on DSs and DEs (III, IV), provides an optimal TSS (II), and automizes the data preparation to increase efficiency (I).

5 Conclusion

In this article, we first collected requirements, formulated an LP model for the TSS problem and, subsequently, built an SSA system that facilitates the application and interpretation of the LP model by BAs that lack data engineering and LP knowledge.

We conducted semi-structured interviews with five BAs and one DS. We identified four key issues in the TSS process, derived TSS criteria, and formulated six requirements on this basis. In the evaluation, we showed that an SSA system has the potential to address identified BAs' key issues in TSS. For future work, we implement the feedback and plan to use ML to leverage expertise about supplier performances [6]. This knowledge base might also ease the parametrization of the LP model.

Acknowledgment. We thank *Mario Nadj* for the fruitful conceptual discussions, and *Pablo Alonso Sanandres,* for supporting our work at **Robert Bosch GmbH**.

References

1. Ho, W., Xu, X., Dey, P.K.: Multi-criteria decision making approaches for supplier evaluation and selection: a literature review. Eur. J. Oper. Res. **202**, 16–24 (2010)
2. Aouadni, S., Aouadni, I., Rebaï, A.: A systematic review on supplier selection and order allocation problems. J. Ind. Eng. Int. **15**(1), 267–289 (2019). https://doi.org/10.1007/s40092-019-00334-y
3. Che, Z.H., Wang, H.S.: Supplier selection and supply quantity allocation of common and non-common parts with multiple criteria under multiple products. Comput. Ind. Eng. **55**, 110–133 (2008)
4. Narasimhan, R., Talluri, S., Mahapatra, S.K.: Multiproduct, Multicriteria model for supplier selection with product life-cycle considerations. Decis. Sci. **37**, 577–603 (2006)
5. Talluri, S.: A buyer–seller game model for selection and negotiation of purchasing bids. Eur. J. Oper. Res. **143**, 171–180 (2002)
6. Forrester Opportunity Snapshot – "Mathematical Optimization and Machine Learning: Your Perfect AI Tech Team", 15 Apr 2022. https://www.gurobi.com/resource/forrester-opportunity-snapshot-mathematical-optimization-and-machine-learning-your-perfect-ai-tech-team/
7. Ocampo, L.A., Abad, G.K.M., Cabusas, K.G.L., Padon, M.L.A., Sevilla, N.C.: Recent approaches to supplier selection: a review of literature within 2006–2016. Int. J. Integr. Supply Manag. **12**, 22–68 (2018)
8. Schuff, D., Corral, K., St. Louis, R.D., Schymik, G.: Enabling self-service BI: a methodology and a case study for a model management warehouse. Inf. Syst. Front. **20**, 275–288 (2018)
9. Michalczyk, S., Nadj, M., Beier, H., Maedche, A.: Designing a self-service analytics system for supply base optimization. In: Nurcan, S., Korthaus, A. (eds.) CAiSE 2021. LNBIP, vol. 424, pp. 154–161. Springer, Cham (2021). https://doi.org/10.1007/978-3-030-79108-7_18
10. Alpar, P., Schulz, M.: Self-service business intelligence. Bus. Inf. Syst. Eng. **58**(2), 151–155 (2016). https://doi.org/10.1007/s12599-016-0424-6
11. Michalczyk, S., Nadj, M., Maedche, A., Gröger, C.: Demystifying job roles in data science: a text mining approach. In: ECIS 2021 Research Papers (2021)
12. Seaman, C.B.: Qualitative methods in empirical studies of software engineering. IEEE Trans. Softw. Eng. **25**, 557–572 (1999)
13. Nielsen, J.: Thinking Aloud: The #1 Usability Tool, 22 Mar 2018. https://www.nngroup.com/articles/thinking-aloud-the-1-usability-tool/
14. Nickel, S., Stein, O., Waldmann, K.-H.: Operations Research. Springer Gabler, Berlin (2014)
15. Ruiz-Torres, A.J., Mahmoodi, F.: The optimal number of suppliers considering the costs of individual supplier failures. Omega **35**, 104–115 (2007)
16. What'sBest! Excel Add-In for Modeling and Optimization, 17 Apr 2022. https://www.lindo.com/index.php/products/what-sbest-and-excel-optimization
17. OR-Tools Google Developers, 15 Apr 2022. https://developers.google.com/optimization

OntoTrace: A Tool for Supporting Trace Generation in Software Development by Using Ontology-Based Automatic Reasoning

David Mosquera[1]([✉]) [iD], Marcela Ruiz[1] [iD], Oscar Pastor[2] [iD], Jürgen Spielberger[1] [iD],
and Lucas Fievet[3]

[1] Zürich University of Applied Sciences, Gertrudstrasse 15, 8400 Winterthur, Switzerland
{mosq,ruiz}@zhaw.ch
[2] PROS-VRAIN: Valencian Research Institute for Artificial Intelligence, Universitat Politècnica
de València, València, Spain
opastor@dsic.upv.es
[3] LogicFlow AG, Butzenstrasse 130, 8041 Zürich, Switzerland
lucas@logicflow.ai

Abstract. Traceability in software development has gained interest due to its
software maintainability and quality assurance benefits. Artifacts such as code,
requirements, mockups, test cases, among others, are feasible trace sources/targets
during the software development process. Existing scientific approaches support
tasks like identifying untraced artifacts, establishing new traces, and validating
existing traces. However, most approaches require input existing traceability data
or are restricted to a certain application domain hindering their practical application. This contemporary challenge in information systems engineering calls for
novel traceability solutions. In this paper, we present OntoTrace: a tool for supporting traceability tasks in software development projects by using ontology-based
automatic reasoning. OntoTrace allows software development teams for inferring
traceability-related data such as i) which are the traceable source/target artifacts;
ii) which artifacts are not yet traced; and iii) given a specific artifact, which are
the possible traces between it and other artifacts. We demonstrate how OntoTrace
works in the context of the Swiss startup LogicFlow AG, supporting the traceability between functional/non-functional requirements and user interface test cases.
We conclude the paper by reflecting on the experience from applying the approach
in practice, and we draw on future challenges and next research endeavors.

Keywords: Software traceability · Ontology · Automatic reasoning · Trace
generation · Software traceability tool

1 Introduction

Traceability in software development refers to creating traces between software artifacts
[1]. A trace is a triplet comprising a source artifact, a target artifact, and a trace link
[2]. Such artifacts include source code, requirements, mockups, test cases, among others. Keeping traceability between software artifacts facilitates quality-assurance-related

J. De Weerdt and A. Polyvyanyy (Eds.): CAiSE Forum 2022, LNBIP 452, pp. 73–81, 2022.
https://doi.org/10.1007/978-3-031-07481-3_9

tasks such as maintenance, verification, and validation tasks, which are regular practices in information systems engineering [3, 4]. In practice, the effort required to maintain, validate, and generate traces between artifacts outweighs traceability benefits [5]. Therefore, some authors propose novel approaches that allow software development teams to create traces between artifacts [5–13]. Although such approaches are helpful, some of them require as input existing traceability data sets or existing traces between artifacts [5, 6, 8, 11], hindering their practical applicability by software development teams that do not currently trace their artifacts. On the other hand, other approaches limit their scope to specific artifacts [7, 9, 10, 12, 13], lacking generality.

In this paper, we propose OntoTrace: an ontology-based automatic reasoning tool for supporting trace generation in software development projects. OntoTrace uses software development teams' context-dependent traceability ontology, representing their specific context source/target artifacts and their traces. Moreover, our approach support software development teams when defining traceability links without relying on historical traceability data sets or limiting their scope to tracing specific software artifacts. Then, software development teams can use OntoTrace to infer traceability-related information such as: i) which are the traceable source/target artifacts; ii) which artifacts are not yet traced; and iii) given a specific artifact, which are the possible traces between it and other artifacts.

To evaluate the feasibility of our approach and exemplify its application, we instantiate our approach in the context of a real-world use case at LogicFlow AG: a Swiss startup that has a traceability gap between functional/non-functional requirements and test scenarios—mainly focused on user interface (UI) test cases. We present the use of OntoTrace by using the LogicFlow AG's traceability ontology, an automatic reasoner, and a graph-like UI to visualize software artifacts and traces. We show that OntoTrace allows for establishing and discovering traceability links. Furthermore, we discuss the next research challenges to a complete technology transference.

The paper is structured as follows: in Sect. 2, we review the related works; in Sect. 3, we set up the running example describing a use case at LogicFlow AG; in Sect. 4, we introduce OntoTrace in the context of our running example; and, finally, in Sect. 5 we discuss conclusions and future work.

2   Related Work

Trace generation and discovery have gained researchers' attention, generating novel and tool-supported approaches. Some authors propose historic-data-based approaches such as artificial neural networks [5, 8], Bayes classifier [13], and similarity-based algorithms [6] for automatically creating traces between artifacts. However, such proposals require large and well-labeled training data sets based on historical traceability data, which are not always available. This represents an entry barrier for software development teams that currently do not trace their artifacts.

On the other hand, some authors propose approaches that do not rely on historical-traceability data sets, such as domain ontology-based recommendation systems [7, 13], pattern languages [9], expert systems [10], and metamodel-based ontologies [12]. Nevertheless, such approaches are limited to generating traces on the specific artifact, lacking generality. Some proposals [7, 8, 10] limit their source/target artifacts to text-based artifacts—e.g., such as textual requirements, source code, and standard norm documents. Therefore, mockups, models, UIs, and other non-textual artifacts are beyond their scope. Similarly, other approaches limit their artifacts to model-based artifacts [12], requirements [9, 13], and source code [9, 11, 13].

To address the gaps mentioned above, we propose an ontology-based automatic reasoning tool named OntoTrace that does not rely on historical-traceability data and is not restricted to a specific set of traceable artifacts. Although some authors base their approach on ontologies [7, 10, 12, 13], the sources describing their proposed ontologies are not available for reusing them. Therefore, OntoTrace also relies on a context-independent traceability ontology, making the sources available for reuse.

3 Running Example: LogicFlow AG Case

In the rest of this paper, we will use as a running example the LogicFlow AG case, a Swiss startup whose main objective is to provide a platform to facilitate the generation of UI testing in software development projects. Currently, LogicFlow AG has a web platform that allows testers to record test scenarios of web-based applications (see Fig. 1). Such test scenarios are automatically transformed into Selenium Script [14], a domain-specific language used for modeling and executing UI test cases. Moreover, LogicFlow AG's platform automatically identifies changes in the UIs, comparing current web-based application version screenshots with former web-based application version screenshots—we refer to this module as UI automatic change identifier (UI-ACI) from now on. Despite the usefulness of the LogicFlow AG platform, startup members have identified that web-based application requirements are hardly traceable to the test scenarios. Such traceability gap hinders the maintainability of test scenarios, increasing the tester's effort to keep them consistent with the requirements. In Fig. 1, we show the LogicFlow AG platform setup and the missing traces between artifacts.

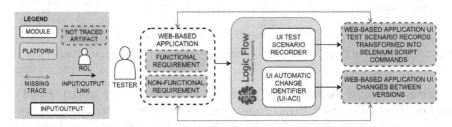

Fig. 1. LogicFlow AG platform setup and missing traces between artifacts.

For instance, a use case where such traceability gap is evident is the following: A Swiss insurance company wants to use the LogicFlow AG platform to generate test scenarios based on their web-based application for calculating insurance premiums. Therefore, the Swiss insurance company's testers create a test scenario based on the company's requirements—i.e., the source artifacts—by using the LogicFlow AG platform. As a result, the testers create one test scenario comprising 63 Selenium Script commands. Moreover, the testers run the test scenario and compare the web-based application versions using the UI-ACI. Then, the LogicFlow AG platform's UI-ACI automatically identifies nine changes in the UI. As a result of using the LogicFlow AG platform, the testers have a set of 72 target artifacts in one test scenario. However, up to this point, the testers do not have any trace between the requirements and the test scenario, hindering the test scenario's maintainability. In Sect. 4, we show how this problematic case can improve by using OntoTrace.

4 OntoTrace: Enabling Ontology-Based Automatic Reasoning for Supporting Trace Generation in Software Development

In this section, we introduce OntoTrace and exemplify it through the running example. OntoTrace allows software development teams to infer traces among software artifacts using ontology-based automatic reasoning. To do so, OntoTrace relies on a domain-independent traceability ontology that has its foundation on general traceability definitions taken from [1, 2, 15], having terms as: trace, artifact, source artifact, target artifact, and traceability link. Therefore, as the first step to using OntoTrace, software development teams should extend such traceability ontology to their specific contexts. We fully extended the traceability ontology to the context of LogicFlow AG, including describing the source artifacts, target artifacts, and the traces between them. However, for the sake of space, in this paper, we show an excerpt of such extension (see Fig. 2).

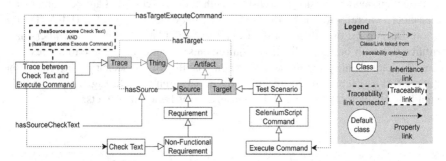

Fig. 2. Excerpt of the OntoTrace traceability ontology extension in the context of LogicFlow AG.

First, we extend the traceability ontology's *source and target* artifacts based on the LogicFlow AG context, having *requirements* as *source artifacts* and *test scenarios* as *target artifacts*. We continue increasing the class hierarchy until we identify two artifacts: *non-functional requirement check texts* as *source artifacts* and *SeleniumScript execute commands* as *target artifacts*. *Check text* is a non-functional requirement that checks if a text in a UI matches a specific format, font, or size. On the other hand, LogicFlow AG testers use the *SeleniumScript execute command* to verify such non-functional requirements in a test scenario. Thus, the *trace between check text and execute command* arises between these artifacts.

Having defined the traceability ontology extension to a specific context, software development teams should use a computational-readable knowledge representation language as OWL (Ontology Web Language) [16] to describe such extended ontology.

Software development teams can use OWL editors such as Protégé [17] to generate an OWL file describing the ontology. This OWL file is the primary input to use OntoTrace. Then, OntoTrace process the OWL file containing the context-dependent ontology by using three main modules: i) the automatic reasoner, ii) the SPARQL query engine, and iii) the trace graph-like visualizer (see Fig. 3).

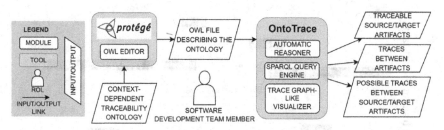

Fig. 3. OntoTrace overview.

To develop the OntoTrace modules, we use Apache Jena [18], a free-open-source Java framework for building ontology-based applications. Apache Jena allows us to integrate and develop the first two OntoTrace modules: the automatic reasoner and the SPARQL query engine. We select Pellet [19] as the OWL-based reasoner, allowing for inferring traceability-related data automatically from the context-dependent ontology. Then, we design a set of SPARQL queries to access the inferred data from the automatic reasoner. Apache Jena provides a default SPARQL query engine to execute such queries. For the sake of space, we do not show the SPARQL queries in this paper. However, we create a public GitHub repository[1] containing all the OWL files with the traceability ontology, the SPARQL queries, and the source code of OntoTrace.

After executing the SPARQL queries, the SPARQL query engine retrieves text-formatted triplets. However, we noticed that having just text-based information hinders the tool's usability. Therefore, we create a graph-like visualizer by using JgraphX [20] that allows software development teams for visualizing the following information: i) all the source/target artifact; ii) which artifacts are untraced; ii) possible traces between artifacts resulting from the automatic reasoning; and iv) the existing traces between artifacts. Thus, OntoTrace allows software development teams to generate traces between artifacts by using the information inferred through ontology-based automatic reasoning.

We test OntoTrace by using the Swiss insurance company use case in the context of LogicFlow AG. In the current status of OntoTrace, we manually create the source artifact individual instances, describing the functional and non-functional requirements. We do the same with the target artifacts, creating the individual instances that describe the test scenario. We manually populate all the ontology with individuals since OntoTrace is not yet integrated with the LogicFlow AG platform. However, in further versions of OntoTrace, we will automate populating the ontology individuals. After creating such individual instances, OntoTrace allows testers to generate the traces between the requirements and the test scenario based on the automatic reasoner inferred information.

---

[1] https://github.com/DavidMosquera/TraceabilityOntology.

We show in Fig. 4 an excerpt of such information regarding the Swiss insurance company use case, showing the possible traces between a *non-functional requirement check text* and *target artifacts* in the *test scenario*.

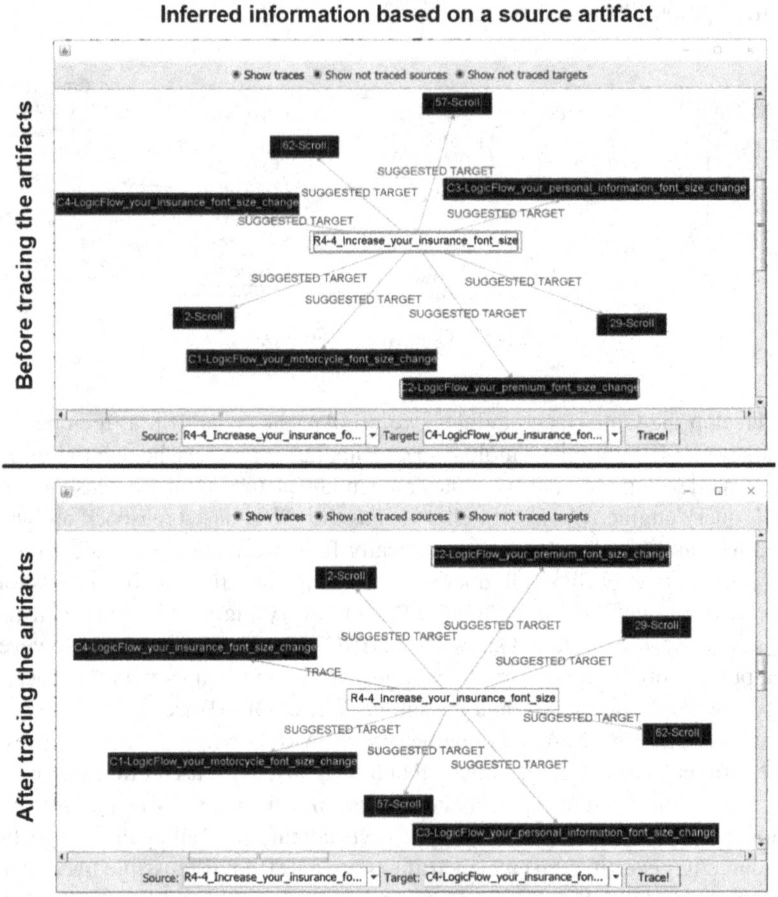

Fig. 4. Excerpt of OntoTrace showing the inferred use case information, representing the source artifacts as white boxes and the target artifacts as black boxes.

In the LogicFlow AG use case, LogicFlow testers using OntoTrace access the artifact suggestions based on the possible traceability links defined into the context-dependent traceability ontology. If the testers manually/automatically add, delete, or edit the traceability links contained in the context-dependent ontology, the OntoTrace suggestions will change. Thus, OntoTrace facilitates the evolution of traceability links without modifying existing traces, SPARQL queries, or the definition of artifacts, thanks to its ontology definition and automatic reasoning.

Although OntoTrace facilitates the evolution of such traceability links, this also causes the number of suggestions to increase over time. Such increasing could affect the scalability of OntoTrace in the long run since the more possible traceability links are established, the more possible traces can exist between source and target artifacts. As part of our future work we plan to investigate how to mitigate this limitation by integrating OntoTrace with functionalities that allow it to generate traces between artifacts automatically. That includes integration with proposals from the literature, such as those reviewed in Sect. 2.

On the other hand, creating artifacts manually, as we did in the LogicFlow use case, is time-consuming. Therefore, we propose that OntoTrace allows automatic generation of artifact instances in the future. We could achieve such automatic generation by using previously defined ontologies. For example, some proposals ontologically describe close-to-natural language requirements, such as user stories [21]. Such already existent ontologies can facilitate the automatic generation of artifact instances inside the context-dependent ontology.

5   Conclusions and Further Work

Trace generation between software development artifacts benefits quality assurance and software maintenance [3, 4]. However, the effort required to generate such traces outweighs traceability-related benefits [5]. In this paper, we reviewed some approaches in the literature for supporting trace generation. Although such approaches are helpful, we observed some of them require historical traceability data, hindering their implementation by software development teams that do not currently trace their artifacts. On the other hand, some approaches lack generality, limiting the set of possible traceable artifacts. Consequently, in this paper, we proposed an ontology-based automatic reasoning tool for supporting trace generation named OntoTrace, which addresses the gaps mentioned above.

OntoTrace requires that software development teams extend a traceability ontology based on general traceability definitions in the literature to their software development context. Thus, software development teams describe context-dependent artifacts such as requirements, source code, test cases, among others, and the traces between them. Then, software development teams can use such ontology together with OntoTrace to automatically infer traceability information such as: i) which are the traceable source/target artifacts; ii) which artifacts are not yet traced; and iii) given a specific artifact, which are the possible traces between it and other artifacts. In this paper, we showed how OntoTrace is successfully implemented by using a running example: a Swiss startup named LogicFlow AG aiming to fulfill the traceability gap between functional/non-functional requirements and UI test cases.

As future research steps, we expect to extend OntoTrace in other directions. As the first remark, OntoTrace depends on several external tools such as Protégé, Pellet, and JgraphX. In practice, we should provide a workspace that integrates all the OntoTrace functionalities, aiming to automate steps of our approach, e.g., automatically creating individual instances. Moreover, as traces between artifacts evolve, we will include new techniques—such as machine learning algorithms—for automatically devising new traceability links while the software development team uses OntoTrace. Such techniques will support software development teams to maintain the context-dependent traceability ontology over time. Finally, other steps such as the user interaction design and empirical validation should be performed in future research endeavors.

Acknowledgments. This work is supported by the Zürich University of Applied Sciences (ZHAW) – School of Engineering: Institute for Applied Information Technology (InIT); and the Innosuisse Flagship Initiative - Project SHIFT. Moreover, we would like to thank LogicFlow AG for collaborating with us on providing data, time, and ideas during the development of this research.

References

1. Charalampidou, S., Ampatzoglou, A., Karountzos, E., Avgeriou, P.: Empirical studies on software traceability: a mapping study. J. Softw. Evol. Process. **33** (2021)
2. Cleland-Huang, J., Gotel, O., Zisman, A.: Software and Systems Traceability. Springer, London (2012)
3. Antoniol, G., Canfora, G., de Lucia, A.: Maintaining traceability during object-oriented software evolution: a case study. In: Proceedings IEEE International Conference on Software Maintenance - 1999 (ICSM 1999), pp. 211–219. IEEE (1999)
4. Sundaram, S.K., Hayes, J.H., Dekhtyar, A., Holbrook, E.A.: Assessing traceability of software engineering artifacts. Requirements Eng. **15**, 313–335 (2010)
5. Lin, J., Liu, Y., Zeng, Q., Jiang, M., Cleland-Huang, J.: Traceability transformed: generating more accurate links with pre-trained BERT models. In: 2021 IEEE/ACM 43rd International Conference on Software Engineering (ICSE), pp. 324–335. IEEE (2021)
6. Javed, M.A., UL Muram, F., Zdun, U.: On-demand automated traceability maintenance and evolution. In: Capilla, R., Gallina, B., Cetina, C. (eds.) ICSR 2018. LNCS, vol. 10826, pp. 111–120. Springer, Cham (2018). https://doi.org/10.1007/978-3-319-90421-4_7
7. Huaqiang, D., Hongxing, L., Songyu, X., Yuqing, F.: The research of domain ontology recommendation method with its applications in requirement traceability. In: 2017 16th International Symposium on Distributed Computing and Applications to Business, Engineering and Science (DCABES), pp. 158–161. IEEE (2017)
8. Guo, J., Cheng, J., Cleland-Huang, J.: Semantically enhanced software traceability using deep learning techniques. In: 2017 IEEE/ACM 39th International Conference on Software Engineering (ICSE), pp. 3–14. IEEE (2017)
9. Javed, M.A., Stevanetic, S., Zdun, U.: Towards a pattern language for construction and maintenance of software architecture traceability links. In: Proceedings of the 21st European Conference on Pattern Languages of Programs, pp. 1–20. ACM, New York (2016)
10. Guo, J., Cleland-Huang, J., Berenbach, B.: Foundations for an expert system in domain-specific traceability. In: 2013 21st IEEE International Requirements Engineering Conference (RE), pp. 42–51. IEEE (2013)
11. Nagano, S., Ichikawa, Y., Kobayashi, T.: Recovering traceability links between code and documentation for enterprise project artifacts. In: 2012 IEEE 36th Annual Computer Software and Applications Conference, pp. 11–18. IEEE (2012)
12. Narayan, N., Bruegge, B., Delater, A., Paech, B.: Enhanced traceability in model-based CASE tools using ontologies and information retrieval. In: 2011 4th International Workshop on Managing Requirements Knowledge, pp. 24–28. IEEE (2011)
13. Hayashi, S., Yoshikawa, T., Saeki, M.: Sentence-to-code traceability recovery with domain ontologies. In: 2010 Asia Pacific Software Engineering Conference, pp. 385–394. IEEE (2010)
14. Selenium - Domain Specific Language. https://www.selenium.dev/documentation/guidelines/domain_specific_language/. Accessed 29 Nov 2021

15. Guo, J., Monaikul, N., Cleland-Huang, J.: Trace links explained: an automated approach for generating rationales. In: 2015 IEEE 23rd International Requirements Engineering Conference (RE), pp. 202–207. IEEE (2015)
16. Web Ontology Language (OWL). https://www.w3.org/OWL/. Accessed 29 Nov 2021
17. Protégé ontology editor. https://www.w3.org/2001/sw/wiki/Protege. Accessed 29 Nov 2021
18. Apache Jena Home Page. https://jena.apache.org/. Accessed 29 Nov 2021
19. Pellet OWL reasoner. https://www.w3.org/2001/sw/wiki/Pellet. Accessed 29 Nov 2021
20. JgraphX github repository. https://github.com/jgraph/jgraphxm. Accessed 29 Nov 2021
21. Thamrongchote, C., Vatanawood, W.: Business process ontology for defining user story. In: 2016 IEEE/ACIS 15th International conference on Computer and Information Science (ICIS), pp. 1–4. IEEE (2016)

Trusting the Big Brother Inside My Pocket: User-Oriented Requirements for Contact Tracing

Claudia Negri-Ribalta[(✉)], Nicolas Herbaut[(iD)], and Camille Salinesi[(iD)]

Centre de Recherche en Informatique, Paris I, France
{claudia-sofia.negri-ribalta,nicolas.herbaut,
camille.salinesi}@univ-paris1.fr

Abstract. Contact tracing (CT) apps have been rolled out as part of combined efforts to control the COVID-19 pandemic. However, these apps haven't been download by the totality of the population, with users raising concerns over the usage of data and data protection. This article analyzes how different app providers and data protection levels can affect the willingness to download a COVID-19 contact tracing app between university students, and if there is a difference between students who downloaded and didn't download the app. Through the usage of a factorial survey experiment (FSE) the paper statistically analyses the data protection and trust (DPT) requirements, using the French COVID-19 CT as a use case. The results show that universities have a positive impact on the trust levels of app providers, while private companies tend to have a negative impact on trust. Subjects also have high expectations on data protection. Our results highlight the importance of data protection and app providers for building trust with users of CT COVID-19 apps.

Keywords: Contact tracing · Trust · Data protection · Requirements · HCI

1 Introduction

COVID-19 related apps were rolled out as part of national plans to control the pandemic by contact tracing. If governments plan on using these apps as part of their efforts for future pandemics, it's pivotal to comprehend data protection and trust (DPT) requirements.

Existing research [2,10,14,15] indicates that users are concerned that these apps might be used for surveillance, hence there are trust conflicts. Yet, some of these studies haven't necessarily worked with statistical analysis or used hypothetical scenarios.

This is an exploratory research, part of a series of DPT articles in the context of information system engineering (ISE). We study the willingness to download COVID-19 contact tracing (CT) apps by university students, and compared

J. De Weerdt and A. Polyvyanyy (Eds.): CAiSE Forum 2022, LNBIP 452, pp. 82–91, 2022.
https://doi.org/10.1007/978-3-031-07481-3_10

between users who did and didn't download the French CT COVID-10 app. The main research question is: How do app providers and data protection affect the willingness to download a COVID-19 contact tracing app?

We expect both app providers and data protection factors to be significant on the willingness to download. App providers which include universities will have higher willingness to download, while higher data protection levels will also have higher willingness to download. We also hypothesize that there is a difference in the coefficient between subjects who downloaded the apps and those who didn't. To gather the data, we used a factorial survey experiment (FSE) which was analyzed with a random intercept mixed multilevel model. FSE is a research tool used in other disciplines, such as sociology [4] and has been occasionally used in RE like in [6,13]. FSE - if correctly designed - can have high internal and external validity. Its high internal validity is a consequence of the experimental variation of the data gathering, which resembles an experiment. Consequently, it can draw conclusions from non-random samples, as different stimuli were presented to the same subject [4]. Its external validity is a consequence of its survey-like characteristics.

This article is a validation and implementation of previous research presented by [13], whose purpose is to help the RE process when dealing with requirements that might have a social bias or ethical requirements. This specific framework proposes the usage of FSE as a tool for the RE activity and highlights that quantitative data can be gathered from different stakeholders - such as users - without necessarily having a random sampling. There has been some history of using FSE in RE, as seen in [6,8]. However, [13] proposed the usage of FSE for RE as a framework, for specific types of requirements. The framework allows the RE practitioner to compare results between different stakeholders. In this case study of CT COVID-19 apps, we compared subjects who download and didn't download the french CT COVID-19 app. Our results suggest these groups have different coefficients in the subjects of interest.

By using the framework proposed by [13], this article not only provides validation and implementation for the specifically cited framework but also provides statistical evidence and analysis on how app providers and data protection can affect the willingness of users to download an app. It also provides evidence that open-source seems to be not that significant in the willingness to download an app.

The paper is divided as follows: Section "2" familiarizes the reader with CT apps and DPT elements. Sect. "3" discusses the research methods used. In Sect. "4", the data is presented, analyzed and discussed. Section "5" analyzes the limitations of this research. Finally, Sect. "6" summarizes the research.

2   Preliminaries and Related Work

Trust. Trust is a concept that spans across multiple areas of our society, and is complex and multidimensional [12]. Due to page limitations, we simply observe that in the literature [1,7,11,12], three elements always appear as decisive for trust: risk, expected behavior and a relationship between two agents. In this paper, we use the definition of trust given by [1]: "trust is the willingness of the trustor to rely on a trustee to do what's promised in a given context, irrespective of the ability to monitor or control the trustee, and even though negative consequences may occur".

Data Protection. For this research, data protection is understood as compliance with the GDPR (CIA principles, data protection by design and default, among others articles).

Privacy and Trust Issues with Contact Tracing Apps. France second CT app, TousAntiCovid, was launched in October 2020 after (among others) criticisms on the privacy of the first version[1]. By June 2021 (we carried our survey between May and June 2021), the app had been downloaded 19 million times[2].

Previous research established the existence of a link between trust in the app provider and willingness to download a Covid-19 CT app [2,5]. [5] suggested that licensing the app with open-source[3] could help with the trust issues.

From a user perspective, data protection, privacy and surveillance concerns have been highlighted across the literature for [2,14,15]. Indeed surveillance and data leaks are specifically mentioned in different studies as a reason for not downloading this app [2,15]. [2] concluded that subjects who have less trust in the government associate the CT apps with surveillance. Furthermore, [2] concludes that even if these apps have perfect privacy and data practices, some subjects might never download them.

3   Research Method

For the study, we followed factorial survey experiment (FSE) research method. FSE has been regarded as a suitable tool to deal with topics that might have social bias [3,13]. FSE has been used to investigate beliefs, attitudes, judgments, or requirements, in a variety of disciplines, ranging from social science to requirement engineering [3,4,6].

3.1   Introduction to Factorial Survey Experiment

In brief, this method consists of presenting the respondents with several scenarios, called vignettes, to be rated them with a defined scale. Each vignette consists on a combination of different factors [4] (elements of interest), each declined into several levels. For example, for 5 factors with 3 levels each, the universe of vignettes is $3 \times 3 \times 3 \times 3 \times 3 = 3^5$.

---

[1] https://reuters.com/article/us-health-coronavirus-france-apps-idUSKBN27A0AZ.

[2] https://data.gouv.fr/fr/datasets/metriques-dutilisation-de-lapplication-tousanticovid/.

[3] As defined in https://opensource.org/docs/osd.

Respondents must rate all or a fraction of vignettes (to avoid fatigue) depending on the design: randomize, decking or design algorithms such as D-efficiency [3]. Since no question is directly prompted, social bias is limited. Because the same respondent rated several related scenarios, causal relationships between variables can be investigated [3].

L1 analysis investigates relations between vignettes, while L2 analysis focuses on how different groups rate similar vignettes. Different statistical model can be used: OLS, mixed multilevel with random intercept (R.I.) or random slope (R.S.), etc.

Due to the intentional variability of the variables inside the survey, FSE resembles an experiment, having high internal validity if properly designed [3]. Although random sampling is desirable due to the external validity, FSE allows generalizing its conclusions as they are a reaction to the experimental stimuli rather than the sampling [4]. In other words, it acts as an experiment too, and conclusion can be made even without random sampling. "The experimental logic of an FS has the advantage of permitting general conclusion about causal mechanism using non-random" [4, pg. 11].

Table 1. Vignette factors and their levels in the survey

Factor	Levels	Detail of factor levels
App provider ($AP)	7	Any combination between government, university, private company
Data protection ($DP)	3	High, basic, little
Open source ($OS)	2	Open source code, proprietary code

3.2 Design of the Study

Factors Definition and Their Levels. The research focuses on DPT and open-source. Table 1 shows the factors and the levels. The factors were carefully worded to avoid including societal values. For example, privacy is usually perceived as an important value, therefore it was defined using the GDPR, rather than privacy. A vignette was of the form 'How comfortable would you feel while downloading a COVID-19 contact tracing application that is $OS, with $DP data protection and was created by $AP?'

Survey Presentation and Testing. The vignette universe size of this study is 42, a number too high for respondents to evaluate. The vignette universe was divided in two decks, based on open-source and each subject was presented 21 vignettes, that could be rated in an 11-Likert scale.

The survey was pre-tested with 80 participants. Feedback made us adapt the presentation of the scenarios into a "table like" form. Our universe of interest is university students in France (2.7 million students). Using Cochran's formula, with a 95% confidence and a 5% margin of error, the desired sample size was of 385 answers.

Given the pandemic, it was difficult to gather a random sample from around France, as mobility was limited. Furthermore, clustering different cities would be difficult due to movement restrictions and universities shutdown. Thus it was decided to grab the sample from students from Paris, understanding the impacts on the external validity. As explained in Sect. 3, due to the internal validity of FSE, results of this study are still significant and interesting, even without a random sampling and even possible biases.

4   Results and Analysis

434 persons answered the survey between May and June 2021, with 414 valid answers (12 rushers, 10 failed the attention test, 7 not studying in Paris were discarded). Only 3 students in Agricultural science answered, and they were deleted as it was not statistically significant. The final dataset has answers from 210 females and 204 males. 231 (56%) respondees answered they had downloaded TousAntiCovid, while 183 (44%) indicated they hadn't. 163 students were from engineering or technology, 89 from social science, 75 from natural science, 56 from humanities and 32 from medical science.

After cleaning the data, we ran a χ^2 test of independence with an alpha of 0.05 and a Bonferroni correction, between the following variables: download, area of study, knowledge of open-source, gender, and last usage of the application. We fail to reject all the H0 of association (independence) between variables.

4.1   Multilevel Model

Following the FSE literature, the data is analyzed using a random intercept multilevel mixed model, based on the reference book [4]. The model is presented in Eq. (1), which is a formalization of the model used to analyze our data.

In Eq. (1), each vignette i is rated by subject t. The factors \$DP and \$AP are evaluated through the beta-coefficient, as they are within-subject variables. \$OS and \$dwn are evaluated through the gamma coefficient, as they are between-subject variables. Citing [4], "X represents the p vignette dimension, Z represents the q response variables". μ is the error added by the fact that subjects rate several vignettes, and ε is the random component. The random intercept is "the sum of the intercept and this error component [i.e., $\beta_0 + \mu_t$]" [4, pg. 89].

$$Y_{it} = \beta_0 + \beta_1 X_{it1} + \beta_2 X_{it2} + \ldots + \beta_p X_{itp} + \gamma_1 Z_{t1} + \gamma_2 Z_{t2} + \ldots + \gamma_q Z_{tq} + \mu_t + \varepsilon_{it} \quad (1)$$

We fitted the equation to our model in different specialized software. The results presented here are obtained from clmm function from ordinal package from R. The clmm runs a cumulative linked mixed model fitted with the Laplace approximation. Different models were tested and compared based on their AIC, log-likelihood and others parameter.[4]

---

[4] Codes and database are available at https://github.com/csnegri/CaiseForum_22_ Negri.

4.2 Analysis

The results show that the different levels of $DP and $AP are statistically significant in the willingness of downloading, but not $OS. The analysis also shows that there are some differences between subjects who did and didn't download the app.

Table 2. Multilevel models, compared by L2 groups ($dwn). Bold elements have different p-values for each L2 group

Term			RI with L2 $Dwn Coef. (s.e.) [IC 95%]	RI for those who downloaded app Coef. (s.e.) [IC 95%]	RI for those who didn't download app Coef. (s.e.) [IC 95%]
Data protection					
High (ref.)			-	-	-
Medium			−1.273 (0.049)*** [−1.369 ; −1.178]	−1.287 (0.064)*** [−1.416 ; −1.161]	−1.282 (0.002)*** [−1.286 ; −1.278])
Low			−2.906 (0.057)*** [−3.018 ; −2.793]	−3.060 (0.076)*** [−3.209 ; −2.910]	−2.714 (0.003)*** [−2.721 ; −2.708])
App provider					
Gov.	Uni.	Priv.			
✓		(ref.)	-	-	-
	✓		0.662 (0.075)*** [0.516 ; 0.808]	0.336 (0.099)*** [0.143 ; 0.529]	1.077 (0.003)*** [1.071 ; 1.084])
		✓	−1.947 (0.079)*** [−2.101 ; −1.794]	−2.328 (0.103)*** [−2.530 ; −2.126]	−1.441 (0.003)*** [−1.254 ; −1.241])
✓		✓	−1.483 (0.075)*** [−1.631 ; −1.338]	−1.681 (0.099)*** [−1.877 ; −1.487]	−1.248 (0.003)*** [1.2549 ; −1.241])
✓	✓		0.390 (0.073)*** [0.246 ; 0.534]	**0.210** (0.098)* [−0.019 ; 0.402]	**0.610** (0.003)*** [0.605 ; 0.615])
	✓	✓	−1.055 (0.074)*** [−1.200 ; −0.910]	−1.373 (0.098)*** [−1.565 ; −1.180]	−0.647 (0.002)*** [−0.651 ; −0.642])
✓	✓	✓	−0.877 (0.074)*** [−1.022 ; −0.723]	−1.061 (0.098)*** [−0.704 ; −0.328]	−0.658 (0.002)*** [−0.663 ; −0.653])
Type of code					
Open source (ref.)			-	-	-
Proprietary code			−0.028 (0.156) [−0.333 ; 0.277]	−0.018 (0.217) [−0.442 ; 0.408]	−0.139 (0.191) [−0.515 ; 0.237]
Download					
No (ref.)			-	-	-
Yes			**1.673** (0.231)*** [1.220 ; 2.125]	-	-
Intercept variance, ID (st.dev)			5.235 (2.288)	4.89 (2.211)	5.711 (2.39)
Respondents			414	231	183
Log likelihood			−15902	−9265	−6594

Significant p-values : o p <0.1 * p <0.05, ** p <0.01, *** p <0.001

Impact of Different App Provider in Willingness to Download. The analysis from the model supports the hypothesis that $AP is significant in the willingness to download. Table 2 shows that app providers that include private companies have consistently negative beta coefficients on average, whereas app providers that include universities - without private companies - are consistently rated with a positive beta coefficient. *University* and *university and government* levels were evaluated at 0.662 and 0.390 points higher on average. In comparison, the levels that included private companies were all rated negatively on average All these results are statistically significant.

The $OS factor has no statistical significance at the different level (*proprietary code*). The subjects rated the level *proprietary code* on average -0.028 points. It may suggest that for the subjects the difference between open source and proprietary is not be critical.

The Impact of Different Data Protection Levels in the Willingness to Download. The analysis reveals that $DP is an important factor for the subjects. For instance, the beta coefficient of medium and low $DP are rated at -1.273 points and -2.906 points lower accordingly. The level *low* of $DP is the highest beta coefficient of all the levels in the study. Previous literature indicates that data protection was a topic that subjects would consistently mention when asked about downloading or not downloading CT apps [2,14].

Difference Between Users Who Did and Didn't Download a French CT COVID-19 App. Both groups gave importance to $DP. Indeed, the factor level of *low data protection* has the biggest beta coefficient of all the levels in the study, rated on average -3.060 and -2.714 points lower in each group. The data suggest that subjects who haven't downloaded such apps place a bit more importance on this requirement.

Moving into $AP, there are difference between both groups. There is a difference in the effect of the involvement of *universities and government* and *universities* in the providence of app. For subjects who didn't download the app, when the app is provided by *university and government*, the willingness to download is higher compared to those that did download the app. Indeed, the subjects who didn't download show beta coefficients 3 times higher than those who did. Therefore, between subjects who didn't download, universities seem to play a bigger role, compared to subjects who did download.

On the other hand, subjects who did download seem to have a better perception of the government as app providers - as the *universities* beta coefficient isn't as big as compared to those who didn't download - but a lower perception of private companies in the same role, as seen by the beta coefficients. The beta coefficient of *private company* for those who downloaded the app is -2.328 (the worst beta coefficient in the whole factor level) compared to a -1.441 for those who didn't download. The beta coefficient of solely *private company* changes when a university is added, with an increase to -1.373 for those who downloaded the app. Yet, this coefficient is still worse when compared with subjects who didn't download the app, whose beta coefficient at this level is -0.647.

This could also be that those who didn't download have a higher perception of universities.

If just the levels of \$AP at *private company, government and private company university and private company* are taken, it would be safe to conclude that those who did download the app trust private companies less. The beta coefficients when private companies are involved are always negative, and for the subjects who downloaded are bigger when compared to those who didn't download bigger between subjects.

Moving on to \$OS, at both levels (L1 and L2) the gamma coefficients of both groups are not statistically significant. Yet, it is important to note that the beta coefficients between the two groups have different signs. For the group of people who didn't download the app, the beta coefficient of proprietary code is -0.139 whereas for those that did download is 0.018.

Governance. Data protection is a critical requirement for subjects and should be specified to the highest standard when designing an COVID-19 CT app.

The results also let us infer that subjects who have downloaded this app aren't indifferent about their personal data, as both groups have similar beta coefficients. A variable that wasn't measured due to the scope and time of the project was the privacy trade-off phenomenon.

From an app provider perspective, that the app provenance impacts on the willingness to download, particularly if universities are involved. What's interesting is that the involvement of universities seems to have a positive impact in the subjects who didn't download the app, as long as there was no involvement of private companies in the development. Given this results, what specific roles could universities play as app providers? What is it exactly that makes universities a source of trust? These are questions that need further thinking.

Different governance designs could help increase the willingness to download for between those who didn't download a contact tracing app. Based on the data, the p-values and significance of *government and university* changes between subjects who did and didn't download. Between subjects who didn't download, its p-value seems to be smaller and have greater significance.

5 Threats to Validity and Future Work

Previous research suggest that subjects trust more institutions/systems with which they are familiar [9]. Thus, this can help explain why subjects might trust more apps coming from universities, but doesn't explain the difference at the L2 level.

The external validity of this study could be improved with other sampling techniques, taking into account age groups and cultural differences. This article should be understood within its scope, that it was carried out between students from French universities. Also, D-efficient design could be used to select the vignette sample. Finally, more factors and levels could have been added to the vignettes. Future studies could also research why subjects downloaded the apps and explore cultural differences, to further investigate the privacy trade-off phenomenon and research if conclusions travels between societies.

6 Conclusion

This research is an exploratory study of the relationship of DPT with the willingness to download COVID-19 CT apps. The data was collected using the FSE method and analyzed with a random intercept mixed model.

Analysis has shown that app providers and data protection are statistically significant. Furthermore, subjects who downloaded and didn't download give different importance to both data protection and app provider. For those who didn't download, having a *university* (with or without *government*) involved in the creation of the app is statistically significant. Indeed *university's* beta was 0.839, making it the highest positive beta of the whole study. From this, we can infer that including universities in the providence of apps can have a positive impact on the willingness to download between subjects who didn't download TousAntiCovid.

References

1. Aljazzaf, Z.M., Perry, M., Capretz, M.A.: Online trust: definition and principles. In: 2010 Fifth International Multi-Conference on Computing in the Global Information Technology (2010)
2. Altmann, S., et al.: Acceptability of app-based contact tracing for covid-19: cross-country survey study. JMIR mHealth uHealth **8**(8) (2020)
3. Atzmüller, C., Steiner, P.: Experimental vignette studies in survey research. Methodol. Eur. J. Res. Methods Behav. Soc. Sci. **6** (2010)
4. Auspurg, K., Hinz, T.: Factorial Survey Experiments, vol. 175. Sage Publications (2014)
5. Bano, M., Zowghi, D., Arora, C.: Requirements, politics, or individualism: what drives the success of covid-19 contact-tracing apps? IEEE Softw. **38**(1) (2021)
6. Bhatia, J., Breaux, T.D., Reidenberg, J.R., Norton, T.B.: A theory of vagueness and privacy risk perception. In: 2016 IEEE 24th International Requirements Engineering Conference (RE) (2016)
7. Corritore, C.L., Kracher, B., Wiedenbeck, S.: On-line trust: concepts, evolving themes, a model. Int. J. Hum. Comput. Stud. **58**(6) (2003)
8. Hibshi, H., Breaux, T.D., Broomell, S.B.: Assessment of risk perception in security requirements composition. In: 2015 IEEE 23rd International Requirements Engineering Conference (RE) (2015)
9. Hoff, K.A., Bashir, M.: Trust in automation: integrating empirical evidence on factors that influence trust. Hum. Fact. **57**(3) (2015)
10. Jonker, M., de Bekker-Grob, E., Veldwijk, J., Goossens, L., Bour, S., Rutten-Van Mölken, M.: Covid-19 contact tracing apps: predicted uptake in the Netherlands based on a discrete choice experiment. JMIR mHealth uHealth **8**(10) (2020)
11. Mayer, R.C., Davis, J.H., Schoorman, F.D.: An integrative model of organizational trust. Acad. Manag. Rev. **20**(3) (1995)

12. McKnight, D.H., Choudhury, V., Kacmar, C.: Developing and validating trust measures for e-commerce: an integrative typology. Inf. Syst. Res. (2002)
13. Negri Ribalta, C.: A method to deal with social bias and desirability in ethical requirements. In: Fischbach, J., Condori-Fernández, N., et al. (eds.) Joint Proceedings of REFSQ-2022 Workshops, Doctoral Symposium, and Poster & Tools Track (2022)
14. Simko, L., Calo, R., Roesner, F., Kohno, T.: Covid-19 contact tracing and privacy: studying opinion and preferences (2020)
15. Williams, S.N., Armitage, C.J., Tampe, T., Dienes, K.: Public attitudes towards covid-19 contact tracing apps: a UK-based focus group study. Health Expectations (2020)

Web of Tactile Things: Towards an Open and Standardized Platform for Tactile Things via the W3C Web of Things

Van Cu Pham[1], Quan Khanh Luu[1], Tuan Tai Nguyen[1],
Nhan Huu Nguyen[1], Yasuo Tan[1], and Van Anh Ho[1,2]([⊠])

[1] Japan Advanced Institute of Science and Technology,
1-1 Asahidai, Nomi, Ishikawa 923-1292, Japan
{cupham,quan-luu,tuan-nguyen,nhnhan,ytan,van-ho}@jaist.ac.jp
[2] Japan Science and Technology Agency, PRESTO, Kawaguchi, Saitama, Japan

Abstract. Toward the development of the Tactile Internet beyond the 5G era and the recently-introduced *Metaverse*, a need for standardized platforms to exchange haptics information for human and cyber-physical systems is emerging. This paper introduces our attempt for an open and standardized platform for tactile things, namely Web of Tactile Thing (WoTT). The WoTT extends the W3C Web of Things (WoT) to exchange haptic information from tactile sensing devices to cross-domain services via already proven Web technologies. This paper proposes (i) haptic vocabularies to generate the WoT Thing Description for vision-based tactile sensing devices, as well as (ii) mechanisms to connect, update, and exchange tactile information efficiently. To prove the feasibility of the platform, a proof of concept includes (i) a tactile sensing device to produce tactile information and (ii) a WoT client that consumes proposed vocabularies to create a digital twin of the physical device, have been implemented. The feasibility of the proposed platform has been verified by abilities to reproduce the digital twin and reflect touch events timely and correctly via the WoTT.

Keywords: Web of Tactile · Tactile Internet · Tactile interoperability

1 Introduction

Nowadays, comprehensive understanding of human behaviours and external environment is the main goal toward the realization of intimate human-machine interactions and tele-operation services. Of numerous sensing modalities, touch, recently, has been attracted many attentions, due to its intrinsic ability to reveal high-fidelity feedback on direct physical interactions with environment [1]. Smart

V. C. Pham, Q. K. Luu, T. T. Nguyen and N. H. Nguyen—Authors are equally contributed.

J. De Weerdt and A. Polyvyanyy (Eds.): CAiSE Forum 2022, LNBIP 452, pp. 92–99, 2022.
https://doi.org/10.1007/978-3-031-07481-3_11

devices embedded with soft artificial skins, here refers to as *tactile sensing devices* are the key enablers for collecting rich tactile information, that can reach human capabilities of sensing physical contact forces and pressures on the entire body. We envisage that tactile sensing devices, in the next few years, will exist in every consumer products, ranging from large-scale pieces of furniture (bed, sofa), to compact wearable devices, and even to tactile robotics [2]. Therefore, an open and standard platform to enable the seamless interoperability of the diverse tactile devices and applications is a crucial question that needs to be addressed in the early stage toward the of the Tactile Internet (Fig. 1).

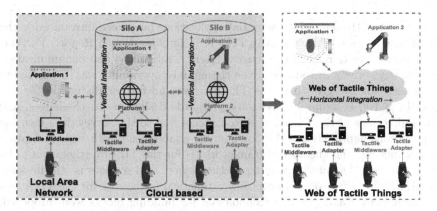

Fig. 1. Web of Tactile Things (WoTT): Breaking incompatible silos for Tactile Things towards the implementation of the Tactile Internet. Our goal is to utilize the horizontal integration at the platform level to counter the fragmentation for the Tactile Internet

In this paper, we propose an extension/plugin of the World Wide Web (W3C) **Web of Things** (WoT) ecosystem that supports tactile sensing devices to pave the way for an open and standardized platform, named *Web of Tactile Things (WoTT)*, for interconnecting tactile devices, exposing tactile data to applications or services via the Web paradigm. The WoT is currently utilized at multiple smart infrastructure areas such as industrial [9], smart buildings [5], smart cities, retails, healthcare, etc. The semantic enabler of the WoT is the *Thing Description* (TD), which can map any physical thing into a *WoT Thing* so that human and machines can understand and interact easily with it via sets of standardized APIs[1].

This WoTT is supposed to bring the simplicity, openness, and success of today Web towards the Tactile Internet. As the very first step, we particularly focused on supporting vision-based tactile sensing devices previously reported in [4], that have high spatial resolution with low sampling rate. Such devices are highly scalable, and pleasure to physical contact, thanks to its inherent soft, continuous skin.

---

[1] https://www.w3.org/TR/wot-scripting-api/.

Main contributions of this work include:

- Proposing an **information model** to implement semantic interoperability for tactile sensing devices via *WoT Thing Description*.
- Proposing a **platform** for tactile sensing devices and services via the semantic abstraction of the W3C WoT.
- Implementing a **use-case** for the W3C WoT towards the development of the Tactile Internet.

2   Related Work

The concept of the TI and its potential applications have been introduced in the ITU-T was introduced in the 2014 ITU-T Technology Watch Report. Furthermore, requirements related to security, latency, reliability, and communication network were briefly introduced. Even though interoperability was mentioned to be an issue for the growth of the TI, there was no further discussion for this issue. In [3,10], a comprehensive survey regards design issues, challenges, and future directions of the TI was reported. According to the survey, it is focusing on proposing haptic codecs [11] for devices, enabling network/communication technologies [6], and theoretical framework [7] for the TI. Nevertheless, a practical framework for interconnecting tactile devices and services is still missing. The *ASSIST-IoT*[2] project is proposing a practical framework for the TI. A layered architecture and possible technologies for building blocks were proposed. Moreover, an open and standardized API for data sharing and application developments is desired but not yet proposed in the current state of the platform.

3   WoT Thing Description for Tactile Devices

An information model, which is compliant with the WoT TD, is essential to bring tactile devices and services into the WoT world. In this section, a tactile thing description (TDD), which is the most important part of the WoTT platform, is designed and implemented. The TDD supports two following interaction affordances:

- **Property Affordance** encapsulates physical aspects of typical vision-based tactile sensing devices, which especially focuses on the description of functional sensing elements characterized by the compliant/soft elastomeric skins. The goal is to digitalize all characteristics of any physical tactile device and make this digital twin accessible via WoT semantic abstraction.
- **Event Affordance** provides a mechanism to notify tactile events to registered applications/ services. By utilizing this affordance, touch related events are automatically notified by lightweight data packets just like an ordinary sensors.
- **Action Affordance** could be extended to reflect behaviors of actuators for a broader type of tactile devices in the future.

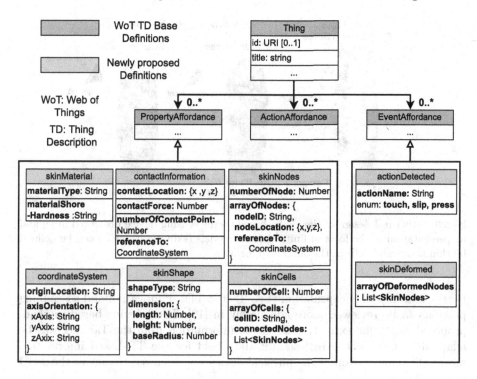

Fig. 2. The overall concept of the Tactile Thing Description

In scope of this paper, a minimal version of the TDD which supports vision-based tactile sensing devices was proposed. Vocabularies and terms of the TDD is self explanatory and are summarized as in Fig. 2.

4 Proof of Concept Implementation

The proof-of-concept (PoC) of the WoTT platform (See Fig. 4), which interconnects and exchanges tactile information between a physical tactile sensing device and its digital twin, was implemented and released as an open-source solution[3]. We will describe the setup and experiment results of the PoC in this section.

4.1 Soft Vision-Based Tactile Sensing Device

Here, we make use of our previous vision-based tactile sensor (named as TacLink) introduced in [4,12], which records the motion of markers on the inner skin surface to infer tactile information, as a showcase for WoTT platform. Figure 3 illustrates structural design of TacLink and its decomposition into different meshes

---

2 https://assist-iot.eu/.
3 https://github.com/Ho-lab-jaist/WoTT.

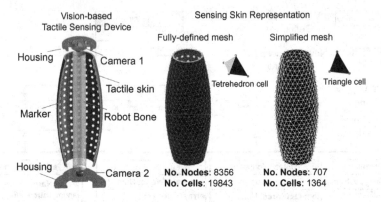

Fig. 3. Structural design of the vision-based tactile sensing device presented in [4] and its presentation in the form of finite element models (skin mesh) which can be defined by skin nodes and cells in the simplified form.

for the data model encapsulation (*i.e.*, Tactile TD). Fabrication and assembling process can be reviewed more adequately in [12]. The learning-based method, proposed in [4], for extraction of tactile information from the TacLink was be adapted to provide the real sensing data field for the TD-based information model. The digitization of the physical device was achieved thanks to the TDD in Sect. 3.

4.2 Software: WoTT Thing Producer (Server)

A WoTT middleware acts as a server that connects the physical tactile sensing device into the WoTT platform in order to exchange tactile information produced by the device. The middleware is implemented in Python utilizing the *wotPY*[4] library to cover the W3C WoT run-time, WoT Scripting API, and protocol bindings (*e.g.*, HTTP, Websocket). As the initialization process, a digital form of the physical device was encoded and provided via *properties* of the TDD. During normal operation, events such as touching the physical devices, an so on, will be emitted to interested clients via predefined *events* of the TDD.

4.3 Software: WoTT Thing Consumer (Client)

A WoTT client was implemented in order to make use of tactile information from the *server* to reproduce a digital twin (static and dynamic information) of the device. As for the initialization, the client consumes the TDD and visualizes encoded information. Moreover, the client also subscribes to tactile events and reflect the event via a 3D model of the tactile sensing device.

---

[4] https://github.com/agmangas/wot-py.

5   Evaluation

5.1   Tactile Thing Description Validity and Bench-Marking

First, the TDD was tested by the validation tool maintained by the W3C WoT Working Group[5]. The TDD and the TDD loaded with tactile information was validated and no problem was found. Then, a bench-marking tool, namely *test-bench* [8], which was developed by the Technical University of Munich has been utilized to further verify interactions with the TDD. As the result, we received a **100%** passed result for every test cases. These results guarantee the validity and correct operations of the TDD in the WoTT platform.

5.2   End-to-End Latency of Reproducing the Digital Twin

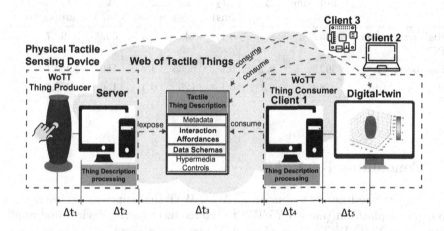

Fig. 4. The overview of the PoC setup: a soft vision based tactile sensing device, a middleware (Server), and applications to represent its digital twin (Client)

The end-to-end latency was evaluated by an experiment of measuring the total time for processing, transmitting tactile data and visualizing a digital twin of the physical tactile sensing device via the WoTT platform via **Local Area Network** (LAN). The necessary time of each step of a complete process is presented in Fig. 4, where Δt_1 is the time for the touch signal to reach the middleware, Δt_2 is the time needed for server to produce the TDD, Δt_3 is the time for network communication, Δt_4 is the time needed for a client to consume the TDD, and Δt_5 is the time taken to visualize the digital twin. The experiment was performed by a human touching the physical device and it was conducted ten times. The end-to-end latency is summarized in Table 1.

---

[5] http://plugfest.thingweb.io/playground/.

According to the results, the time needed to produce and consume the TDD are short (even for a raspberry Pi of **4.9** ms) and does not impact the total end-to-end latency in a perceivable way. For a high-performance PC, the total latency via LAN is approximately **92.7** ms. This number might vary due to network communication, however, this result is promising. For regular PC or embedded devices, a significant amount of time was used for network communication and visualization parts. However, visualization will not be always necessary. In real applications, this visualization process can be replaced by triggering haptic feedback and so on. Therefore, these results are in acceptable range, which proves the feasibility of the WoTT platform in interconnecting tactile sensing devices and applications.

Table 1. End-to-end latency measurement.

Device	Init. time (ms)	Δt_1 (ms)	Δt_2 (ms)	Δt_3 (ms)	Δt_4 (ms)	Δt_5 (ms)	End-to-end latency (ms)
High-performance PC	652	8.1	0.1	14.3	0.3	69.9	92.7
Raspberry Pi	3921	8.1	0.1	6665	4.9	1608	8286.1
Regular laptop	782	8.1	0.1	125	0.4	150	283.6

6   Concluding Remarks

This paper introduces an extension for W3C WoT that supports tactile devices to create a platform (named WoTT) to interconnect tactile devices and applications via W3C WoT abstractions. We introduce a novel information model to map physical tactile sensing devices into digital forms and it can represent all characteristics and events (human interactions) of physical devices. The proposed information model was validated by tools provided by W3C WoT Working Group/Interest Group members. To prove the feasibility of our solution, we conduct an experiment that uses a physical tactile sensing device and a digital twin of it. We were able to reproduce the physical devices and reflect haptic information via the W3C WoT. The overhead added by the extension is relatively small compared to the benefit that allows Web developers to join and develop applications for the Tactile Internet. In the future, we plan to leverage this approach toward generalized ontology model for tactile sensing devices, implement data transmission with low latency, and evaluate on actual robotic applications using WoTT.

Acknowledgements. This work was fully supported by JST Precursory Research for Embryonic Science and Technology PRESTO under Grant JPMJPR2038.

References

1. Altun, K., MacLean, K.E.: Recognizing affect in human touch of a robot. Pattern Recogn. Lett. **66**, 31–40 (2015). https://doi.org/10.1016/j.patrec.2014.10.016. https://www.sciencedirect.com/science/article/pii/S016786551400333X. Pattern Recognition in Human Computer Interaction
2. Dahiya, R.S., Metta, G., Valle, M., Sandini, G.: Tactile sensing-from humans to humanoids. IEEE Trans. Rob. **26**(1), 1–20 (2010). https://doi.org/10.1109/TRO.2009.2033627
3. Fanibhare, V., Sarkar, N.I., Al-Anbuky, A.: A survey of the tactile internet: design issues and challenges, applications, and future directions. Electronics **10**(17) (2021). https://doi.org/10.3390/electronics10172171. https://www.mdpi.com/2079-9292/10/17/2171
4. Ho, V.A., Nakayama, S.: IoTouch: whole-body tactile sensing technology toward the tele-touch. Adv. Robot. **35**(11), 685–696 (2021). https://doi.org/10.1080/01691864.2021.1925588
5. Ibaseta, D., et al.: Monitoring and control of energy consumption in buildings using wot: a novel approach for smart retrofit. Sustain. Cities Soc. **65**, 102637 (2021). https://doi.org/10.1016/j.scs.2020.102637. https://www.sciencedirect.com/science/article/pii/S2210670720308532
6. Mekikis, P.V., et al.: NFV-enabled experimental platform for 5G tactile internet support in industrial environments. IEEE Trans. Industr. Inf. **16**(3), 1895–1903 (2020). https://doi.org/10.1109/TII.2019.2917914
7. Padhi, P.K., Charrua-Santos, F.: 6G enabled tactile internet and cognitive internet of healthcare everything: towards a theoretical framework. Appl. Syst. Innov. **4**(3) (2021). https://doi.org/10.3390/asi4030066. https://www.mdpi.com/2571-5577/4/3/66
8. Schlott, V.E., Korkan, E., Kaebisch, S., Steinhorst, S.: W-ADE: timing performance benchmarking in web of things. In: Bielikova, M., Mikkonen, T., Pautasso, C. (eds.) ICWE 2020. LNCS, vol. 12128, pp. 70–86. Springer, Cham (2020). https://doi.org/10.1007/978-3-030-50578-3_6
9. Sciullo, L., Bhattacharjee, S., Kovatsch, M.: Bringing deterministic industrial networking to the W3C web of things with TSN and OPC UA. In: Proceedings of the 10th International Conference on the Internet of Things, IoT 2020. Association for Computing Machinery, New York (2020). https://doi.org/10.1145/3410992.3410997
10. Sharma, S.K., Woungang, I., Anpalagan, A., Chatzinotas, S.: Toward tactile internet in beyond 5G era: recent advances, current issues, and future directions. IEEE Access **8**, 56948–56991 (2020). https://doi.org/10.1109/ACCESS.2020.2980369
11. Steinbach, E., et al.: Haptic codecs for the tactile internet. Proc. IEEE **107**(2), 447–470 (2019). https://doi.org/10.1109/JPROC.2018.2867835
12. Van Duong, L., Ho, V.A.: Large-scale vision-based tactile sensing for robot links: design, modeling, and evaluation. IEEE Trans. Rob. **37**(2), 390–403 (2021). https://doi.org/10.1109/TRO.2020.3031251

Mining Fork-Including Software Development Traces

Iris Reinhartz-Berger[1]([⊠]) [iD] and Amir Tomer[2] [iD]

[1] Information Systems Department, University of Haifa, Haifa, Israel
`iris@is.haifa.ac.il`
[2] Software Engineering Department, Kinneret College on the Sea of Galilee, Tzemach, Israel
`tomera@mx.kinneret.ac.il`

Abstract. Open-source software development is a common practice that encourages collaborative development and reuse across projects. Forking is a way to make a copy of an existing project and explore it for different purposes. Two types of forks are commonly mentioned in the literature: *contributing forks* which continue the development lines of the forked projects and aim at merging the contribution back to the forked projects; and *independently developed forks* which open new lines of development deviating from the forked projects. In this study, we aim to explore characteristics of fork-involving traces for better understanding collaboration and reuse considerations in software development. Analyzing 880 Java projects and their related action and observation events, with process mining and statistical techniques, we found that the occurrence of certain event types may predict the fork type, while the creation of certain fork types increase the involvement of users in the forked projects.

Keywords: Forks · Software development · Process mining · Development traces

1 Introduction

Nowadays information systems engineering and software development rely much on collaborative development which enables developers to learn from previously developed artifacts and reuse them. Forking is a well-known mechanism in open source software repositories for collaborative development; it supports the creation of new projects, named *forkees*, from an existing project, named *forked project*. The authors in [1] found high value in forking, especially in contribution to exposing and fixing software bugs and adding new features. In cases that the forked project is further developed and maintained, the literature distinguishes between two types of active forks [2, 6]: *contributing forks* which continue by developing new artifacts that are eventually merged back to the forked project via pull requests; and *independently developed forks* which lead towards a course of independent projects through commits that are unique to the forkees.

Forking is extensively studied. The work in [10], for example, explores the impact of fork type on project sustainability; the work in [8] studies the efficiency of forking

© The Author(s), under exclusive license to Springer Nature Switzerland AG 2022
J. De Weerdt and A. Polyvyanyy (Eds.): CAiSE Forum 2022, LNBIP 452, pp. 100–109, 2022.
https://doi.org/10.1007/978-3-031-07481-3_12

practices. Several works (e.g., [4, 5, 7]) acknowledge the strong correlation between forking and project popularity, shedding light on the practice of forking. However, all these works neglect the behavioral, event-related aspects of forking and collaborative software development. Perceiving open source software repositories as event-driven management systems, we suggest focusing on the operations recorded by their API in order to mine the underlying processes and the features that characterize forking of different types.

In this study, we explored fork-inlcuding traces for better understanding collaboration and reuse considerations in software development. To this end, we analyzed the types of events in such traces, the partial traces *before* the forking operations and the continuation of the traces in the forked projects *after* the forking operations. By doing so, we try to reveal patterns of behavior leading towards (and maybe encouraging) forking, as well as to reveal post-operation patterns of behavior. Accordingly, we address the following research questions:

RQ1. What are the main types of events in open software development environments that support collaborative work?

RQ2. Which types of events lead to the creation of different types of forks in given projects?

RQ3.How does forking of different types influence the involvement of the users in the forked projects after the forking occurred?

The rest of the paper is structured as follows: Sect. 2 introduces a categorization framework for addressing RQ1; Sect. 3 presents the empirical study conducted for addressing RQ2 and RQ3; Finally, Sect. 4 discusses the implications and the threats to validity, while Sect. 5 summarizes the above and highlights some future research directions.

2 Categorizing Software Development Events

To address RQ1, we suggest the conceptual framework depicted in Fig. 1. This framework includes the main types of development events in open software development environments, in particular in GitHub. It further categorizes the events according to two dimensions: the involved elements and the event nature. The involved element may refer to the project itself – REPO[1]; its commits – COMMIT; its issues for suggesting improvements, tasks or questions – ISSUE; and its base pull requests for handling proposed changes – PR. The event nature distinguishes between action and observation: action events modify the information on the involved elements, while observation events add complimentary information and may indicate some user interest in the projects in general and in the specific elements in particular. An additional type of events that gets a special attention in our study is forking, i.e., fork creation – FORK. We concentrate here on contributing and independently developed forks, ignoring inactive forks, namely forks that are not further developed and maintained. Next we present the core definitions of event, trace (a sequence of events made by a *certain user* to a *certain project*) and contributing/independently developed forks.

---

[1] We used REPO for referring to project-related events, to avoid confusion with the general term 'project' which refers to the entire metadata of the software project.

Definition 1: An *event* is a tuple (p, u, ev, t, el, n), where p is the project to which the event belongs, u is the user who performed it, ev is the event (e.g., creating, watching, merging, etc.), t is its timestamp, el ∈ {REPO,COMMIT,PR,ISSUE, FORK} is the element to which the event relates and n ∈ {ACT,OBS} is the nature of the event (action or observation, respectively).

Definition 2: A *trace* is a sequence 'of events $<e_1 \ldots e_n>$ satisfying for each i, j, $e_i.p = e_j.p$ (same project), $e_i.u = e_j.u$ (same user) and $i < j \rightarrow e_i.t < e_j.t$ (sequence in time).

Definition 3: Let p, p' be projects satisfying fork(p, p')[2] and having sets of development events E, E', respectively.

- p' is a *contributing fork* if contribute(p', p)[3] holds.
- p' is an *independently developed fork* if it is not contributing and there is e '∈ E' such that e'.el = COMMIT and e'.n = ACT.

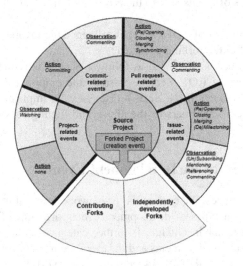

Fig. 1. The suggested framework

In summary, to address RQ1, we categorize the development events along two dimensions: the involved elements (REPO, COMMIT, ISSUE, PR) and the event nature (ACT, OBS), leading to 8 categories of events.

---

[2] fork(p, p') denotes the dependency between the forkee p' and its forked project p.

[3] contribute(p', p) is a predicate indicating whether (or not) the forkee p' contributes to the forked project p via a merging pull request event.

3   Characterizing Fork-Including Software Development Traces

To address the two other research question (RQ2, RQ3), we conducted an empirical study, whose dataset, procedures and results are described below.

3.1   The Dataset

Our dataset is based on GHTorrent, which monitors the Github public event time line [3][4]. For each event, GHTorrent retrieves its contents and their dependencies, exhaustively.

Following observations from related works, and in order to concentrate on projects with significant characteristics relevant to our study, we used all projects satisfying the following conditions: (1) created during the year 2014 and were not deleted (i.e., have 4.5–5.5 years of existence by June 2019) (2) classified as written in Java, and (3) are highly forked (i.e., each yielded at least 100 forkees). Overall, we retrieved 880 projects and 366,631 forkees. After filtering out deleted forkees, we were left with 355,403 forkees to the 880 projects. The forked projects were related to 5,112,603 events of different types, 3,624,658 of which were involved in traces of length longer than 1. We refer to this set as our dataset (see Fig. 2(a) for details).

Characteristic	Value
Overall events	3,624,658
Events related to forked projects	3,507,735
Actions in forked projects	1,756,001 (50.06%)
Observations in forked projects	1,751,734 (49.94%)
Fork creation	116,923
Inactive forks	84,318 (72.11%)
Contributing forks	26,018 (22.25%)
Independently developed forks	6,587 (5.63%)

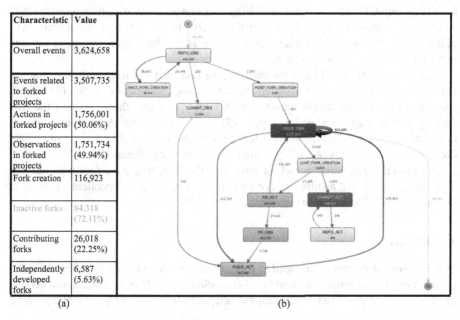

(a)   (b)

Fig. 2. (a) The dataset characteristics; (b) The generated process map

Most events in the dataset (more than 3.5 million) related to the forked projects and almost 117,000 – to fork creation. About half of the events were actions and half had

---

[4] We particularly used the latest MySQL version of GHTorrent, dumped on June 1st, 2019; see https://ghtorrent.org/downloads.html.

an observation nature. Almost half of the events relate to issues, more than a quarter to commits and less than a quarter to pull requests. Finally, most forks were inactive, less than a quarter were contributing, and only 5.63% were used for opening an independent line of development[5].

3.2 Execution and Analysis Procedures

In order to analyze ("directly follows") edges in the relevant traces, we used process mining and particularly Disco software[6]. Figure 2(b) depicts the process map generated for our dataset. As can be seen, *independent fork creation* follows in many (about third) of the cases repository observation and in some cases involvement of the users in the forked projects can be observed (e.g., though issue observation events). *Contributing fork creation* may follow different events, but in many cases (two thirds of the cases), they were associated with active involvement of the users in the pull requests of the forked projects[7]. The process maps also shows *inactive fork creation*, which is quite common. Such creations are frequently associated with repository observation of the forked projects (watching events), either immediately before or immediately after the fork creation.

Grouping the traces according to the involved events and their order, 26,382 variants have been found. We filtered out those having only one occurrence, remaining with 3,392 variants. The maximal length of a trace in those variants was 675, but most of them were of length 2 to 10. Only 1,582 variants included at least one forking operation (37 variants included even 2 to 4 such operations).

For each of the 1,582 relevant variants, we recorded the following information: (1) Identity & occurrence information (variant number, number of cases); (2) Variant characteristics (variant length, number of forking operations, the step when the first forking operation appeared and its type)[8]; (3) Prefix traces (immediate event, numbers of events of each type before the first forking operation); (4) Suffix traces (immediate event, numbers of events of each type after the first forking operation).

We used a multinomial model for analyzing the data, where the fork type was the dependent variable and all other aforementioned features were independent variables in the same model. The factors were tested for $\alpha = 0.05$.

3.3 Results

In the context of the traces that lead to forks (RQ2), we found three significantly influencing factors: the immediate event ($\chi^2(14) = 488.68$, $p < 0.0001$), pull request actions ($\chi^2(2) = 560.70$, $p < 0.0001$) and commit actions ($\chi^2(2) = 12.69$, $p = 0.0018$). These

---

[5] The dataset, as well as its analyses, can be found at https://doi.org/10.5281/zenodo.6351644.

[6] https://fluxicon.com/disco/

[7] Note that these pull request actions refer to the forked projects and are not the merge operations of the forkees into the forked projects, as expected in contributing forks.

[8] Note that although some traces included more than one fork, this was very rare (happened in 37 out of 3,392 variants, and overall in 716 out of 175,414 cases). Hence, we considered in our analyses only the first forking operation in each trace/variant.

results led to the following outcomes. Due to page limitation constraints, Fig. 3(a) visually presents the results only for the immediate event.

Outcome 1. *Contributing forks* are characterized by either:

- Being created as the first communication of the user with the project, without any prior action or observation of the user in the forked project;
- Being created (eventually) after a pull request action in the forked project. In other words, the results show that the probability to have a pull request action in the forked project prior to the creation of a contributing fork is *high*.

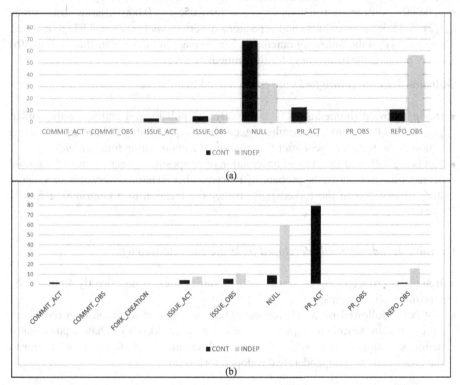

Fig. 3. (a) The dependencies between prefix traces and fork types – immediate (preceding) event; (b) The dependencies between suffix traces and fork types – immediate (following) event

Outcome 2. *Independently developed forks* are characterized by:

- Being created just after repository observation operations (namely, watching events)[9];
- Being created (eventually) after (several) commit actions in the forked project. Actually, the results show that the probability to create an independently developed fork

---

[9] However, this also characterizes inactive forks.

increases as the user performs more commits in the forked project prior to the fork creation.

> These outcomes (RQ2) suggest that contributing fork creation commonly starts user traces or occurs after pull request actions, whereas independently developed forks are commonly created immediately after repository observation operations or subsequently after commit actions.

With respect to the continuation of traces after the first forking operation (RQ3), we found four significantly influencing factors: the immediate event ($\chi^2(14) = 658.87$, $p < 0.0001$), pull request actions ($\chi^2(2) = 1887.05$, $p < 0.0001$), issue observations ($\chi^2(2) = 15.38$, $p = 0.0005$) and repository observations ($\chi^2(2) = 7.82$, $p < 0.02$). These resulted in the following outcomes. Due to page limitation constraints, Fig. 3(b) visually presents the results only for the immediate event.

Outcome 3. *Contributing forks* are characterized by:

- Being followed (immediately or eventually) by pull request actions in the forked project. In other words, the results suggest that the probability to have a pull request action in the forked project after the creation of a contributing fork is *high*;
- Not being followed by an issue observation or a repository observation in the forked project (in other words, the probability to have either an issue observation or a repository observation in the forked project after the creation of a contributing fork is *low*).

Outcome 4. *Independently developed forks* are characterized by:

- Being the last event in the traces, and in some cases, being directly followed by repository observations;
- Not being followed by a pull request action, an issue observation or a repository observation in the forked project (in other words, the probability to have a pull request action, an issue observation or a repository observation in the forked project prior to the creation of an independently developed fork is *low*).

> Our findings (RQ3) suggest that contributing fork creation commonly occurs (immediately or eventually) after pull request actions, whereas independently developed forks are commonly created at the end of traces (i.e., the users stop observing or acting on the forked projects).

4 Discussion and Threats to Validity

Analysis and interpretation of the results in the previous section show that creation of forks may involve the creators (the owners of the forkees) not only in the forkees, but also in the forked projects; this involvement can take place at early stages, before the fork is created, or afterwards. However, there appear to be specific types of events that are more significantly performed than others. Perceiving open source coding as a social activity, users may aim to increase their popularity and encourage the reuse of their code through active forking. Our findings may lead to "best practices" relevant to project owners to disseminate their projects and changes.

Project Dissemination: The reported results suggest that for disseminating projects their owners cannot rely only on the project community (e.g., committers). Watchers indeed tend to create independently developed forks, but the fork creators tend to get involved only after creating (contributing) forks, if at all. In some cases, involvement exists through pull request actions prior to contributing fork creation and through commit actions prior to independently developed fork creation. In these cases, project dissemination can be done also to pull request actors and committers.

Change Dissemination: After forkees have been created, it is important to be aware of the forked project evolution (changes). The owners of the forked projects may be interested in some involvement of the owners of their forkees. Our results suggest that while it is difficult to define the relevant community for independently developed forks, pull request actors may be targeted for this purpose.

Several threats of validity were identified during the study and deserve further consideration. First, we referred only to formal forks created in a single environment GitHub using its interface. The work in [9], for example, extends the definition of fork beyond the one obtained directly from GitHub metadata to forked projects generated on other platforms. Second, we currently investigated the traces individually, as information about actions and consequences are not implicitly available. Future research should explore dependencies among traces belonging to the same users, the same groups, or the same projects. Third, the categorization we suggested consolidates data relevant to the individual events. Further investigation and evaluation of the strengths or weaknesses of our conceptual framework is needed. Finally, the results are limited by the dataset we used and the statistical methods we applied. Although we have not used the specific characteristics of the dataset in the analysis procedure, replication of the study to different datasets is needed to verify generalizability.

5 Summary and Future Research

In this work, we discovered event-related dependencies in fork-including software development traces. To this end, a trace was defined as a sequence of events made by a *certain user* to a *certain project*. We introduced a conceptual framework, in which those events are categorized along two dimensions: the involved elements, namely projects/repositories, commits, base pull requests and issues, and the event nature which distinguishes between action and observation operations. Using this framework, we analyzed potential dependencies between development events and forking, concentrating on contributing and independently developed forks, which support collaborative development and reusing. The analysis used process mining to identify interesting variants and statistical techniques to reveal patterns of behavior. The results were interpreted as "best practices", aiming to assist project owners who aim to utilize the social coding platform to disseminate their projects and changes through forkees.

This work may continue in various further directions. Particularly, we plan to explore interdependencies across traces, especially traces made by users related to each other, either by working in the same organization or collaborating on a number of projects. We also intend to apply additional techniques to the analysis. Machine learning, as one example, may be applied to the process mining results, in addition or alternatively to the statistical analysis, in order to reveal further mutual relations between development and forking events. Another example is text mining which may be applied to certain data items (e.g., issues, comments) in order to find both justifications and considerations which may support user decisions to perform certain operations, on top of the quantitative results.

Acknowledgement. This research is partially supported by the Israel Science Foundation under grant agreements 1065/19.

References

1. Biazzini, M.: "May the fork be with you": novel metrics to analyze collaboration on GitHub. In: Proceedings of the 5th International Workshop on Emerging Trends in Software Metrics, pp. 37–43, June 2014
2. Cosentino, V., Izquierdo, J.L.C., Cabot, J.: A systematic mapping study of software development with GitHub. IEEE Access **5**, 7173–7192 (2017)
3. Gousios, G., Vasilescu, B., Serebrenik, A., Zaidman, A.: Lean GHTorrent: GitHub data on demand. In: Proceedings of the 11th Working Conference on Mining Software Repositories, pp. 384–387, May 2014
4. Jiang, J., Lo, D., He, J., Xia, X., Kochhar, P.S., Zhang, L.: Why and how developers fork what from whom in GitHub. Empir. Softw. Eng. **22**(1), 547–578 (2016). https://doi.org/10.1007/s10664-016-9436-6
5. Nyman, L., Mikkonen, T.: To fork or not to fork: fork motivations in SourceForge projects. Int. J. Open Source Softw. Process. (IJOSSP) **3**(3), 1–9 (2011)
6. Rastogi, A., Nagappan, N.: Forking and the sustainability of the developer community participation – an empirical investigation on outcomes and reasons. In: 2016 IEEE 23rd International Conference On Software Analysis, Evolution, and Reengineering (SANER), vol. 1, pp. 102–111. IEEE, March 2016
7. Robels, G., González-Barahona, J.M.: A comprehensive study of software forks: dates, reasons and outcomes. In: Hammouda, I., Lundell, B., Mikkonen, T., Scacchi, W. (eds.) IFIP International Conference on Open Source Systems, pp. 1–14. Springer, Heidelberg (2012). https://doi.org/10.1007/978-3-642-33442-9_1
8. Teinemaa, I., Dumas, M., Rosa, M.L., Maggi, F.M.: Outcome-oriented predictive process monitoring: review and benchmark. ACM Trans. Knowl. Discovery from Data (TKDD) **13**(2), 1–57 (2019)

Mining Fork-Including Software Development Traces 109

9. Zhou, S., Vasilescu, B., Kästner, C.: What the fork: a study of inefficient and efficient forking practices in social coding. In: Proceedings of the 2019 27th ACM Joint Meeting on
European Software Engineering Conference and Symposium on the Foundations of Software
Engineering, pp. 350–361, August 2019
10. Zhou, S., Vasilescu, B., Kästner, C.: How has forking changed in the last 20 years? A study
of hard forks on GitHub. In: 2020 IEEE/ACM 42nd International Conference on Software
Engineering (ICSE), pp. 445–456. IEEE, October 2020

Temporal Performance Analysis for Block-Structured Process Models in Cortado

Daniel Schuster[1,2]($\boxtimes$) (iD), Lukas Schade[2], Sebastiaan J. van Zelst[1,2] (iD),
and Wil M. P. van der Aalst[1,2] (iD)

[1] Fraunhofer Institute for Applied Information Technology FIT,
Sankt Augustin, Germany
{daniel.schuster,sebastiaan.van.zelst}@fit.fraunhofer.de
[2] RWTH Aachen University, Aachen, Germany
lukas.schade@rwth-aachen.de, wvdaalst@pads.rwth-aachen.de

Abstract. Process mining techniques provide insights into operational
processes by systematically analyzing event data generated during process execution. These insights are used to improve processes, for instance,
in terms of runtime, conformity, or resource allocation. Time-based performance analysis of processes is a key use case of process mining. This
paper presents the performance analysis functionality in the process mining software tool Cortado. We present novel performance analyses for
block-structured process models, i.e., hierarchical structured Petri nets.
By assuming block-structured models, detailed performance indicators
can be calculated for each block that makes up the model. This detailed
temporal information provides valuable insight into the process under
study and facilitates analysts to identify optimization potential.

Keywords: Process mining · Performance analysis · Alignments

1 Introduction

Process mining [1] comprises various methods to systematically analyze event
data that are generated during the execution of operational processes and stored
within organizations' information systems. Analyzing event data offers great
potential for gaining valuable insights into the process under investigation. These
insights are used to improve processes, i.e., the key objective of process mining.

The temporal performance analysis of processes is of major practical relevance, e.g., to determine bottlenecks within processes. This paper presents novel
performance analysis functionality for *block-structured process models* in the tool
Cortado [11]. By focusing on block-structured models, performance indicators
(PIs) can be calculated for each block that makes up the process model individually. Calculating PIs for individual blocks of block-structured models represents
a novelty compared to existing tools, which often only offer performance analysis
per activity in the process model and globally, i.e., for the entire process model.

© The Author(s), under exclusive license to Springer Nature Switzerland AG 2022
J. De Weerdt and A. Polyvyanyy (Eds.): CAiSE Forum 2022, LNBIP 452, pp. 110–119, 2022.
https://doi.org/10.1007/978-3-031-07481-3_13

Table 1. Example of an event log

Event ID	Case ID	Activity label	Start timestamp	Completion timestamp	...
1	1	Activity A	07/13/21 08:00	07/13/21 09:30	...
2	1	Activity B	07/13/21 08:30	07/13/21 11:00	...
3	1	Activity C	07/13/21 09:00	07/13/21 12:00	...
4	1	Activity D	07/13/21 11:30	07/13/21 13:30	...
5	1	Activity E	07/13/21 11:40	07/13/21 13:00	...
6	1	Activity B	07/13/21 14:30	07/13/21 16:00	...
7	1	Activity B	07/13/21 16:30	07/13/21 17:00	...
8	2	Activity A	07/13/21 08:00	07/13/21 09:30	...
9	2	Activity B	07/13/21 09:00	07/13/21 10:00	...
⋮	⋮	⋮	⋮	⋮	⋮

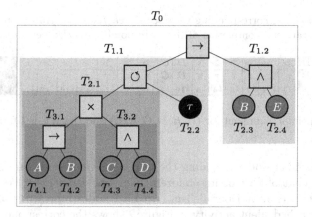

Fig. 1. Example of a process tree T_0. Subtrees are highlighted in gray

In short, Cortado contributes to the state-of-the-art in model-based performance analysis.

The subsequent sections are structured as follows. Section 2 introduces preliminaries. Section 3 presents Cortado's model-based performance analysis approach including various PIs calculated for block-structured models. Section 4 presents related work and tools. Finally, Sect. 5 concludes this paper.

2   Preliminaries

Event data, as considered in process mining [1], describe recorded process executions. Table 1 shows an example of an event log. Each row corresponds to an event capturing the execution of a process activity. Each event is assigned to a case by a case-ID. For instance, the first event in Table 1 shows that activity A was executed on 07/13/21 from 08:00 to 09:30 for case 1. Events assigned the same case-id are also referred to as a *trace*.

Cortado uses *process trees* representing *block-structured* process models that are a subclass of sound Workflow-nets (WF-nets). Figure 1 shows an example

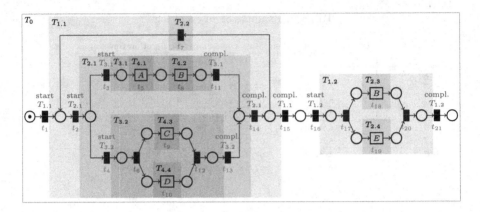

Fig. 2. Workflow net corresponding to process tree T_0. Silent transitions are used to represent the start and completion of the corresponding blocks, i.e., subtrees.

$\gg$	$\gg$	$\gg$	A	B	$\gg$	$\gg$	$\gg$	$\gg$	$\gg$	$\gg$	D	C	$\gg$	$\gg$	$\gg$	$\gg$	$\gg$	$\gg$	E	E	$\gg$	$\gg$	$\gg$
τ	τ	τ	A	B	τ	τ	τ	τ	τ	τ	D	C	τ	τ	τ	τ	τ	τ	E	$\gg$	B	τ	τ
t_1	t_2	t_3	t_5	t_8	t_{11}	t_{14}	t_7	t_2	t_4	t_6	t_{10}	t_9	t_{12}	t_{13}	t_{14}	t_{15}	t_{16}	t_{17}	t_{19}		t_{18}	t_{20}	t_{21}

Fig. 3. Optimal alignment for $\langle A, B, D, C, E, E \rangle$ and the WF-net from Fig. 2

tree T_0. Each inner node, including the root node, represents an operator that specifies the control-flow of its children. Four operators exist: sequence ($\rightarrow$), choice ($\times$), loop ($\circlearrowleft$), and parallelism ($\wedge$). Leaf nodes represent process activities or the so-called silent activity τ. Figure 2 shows the corresponding WF-net, describing the same language as process tree T_0. We use silent transitions (cf. black filled transitions in Fig. 2) to represent the start and completion for each subtree that is not a leaf node. For a formal introduction to process trees and the translation to and from WF-nets and process trees, we refer to [1].

Alignments [2] relate observed process behavior (i.e., event data) with modeled behavior (i.e., a process model). Figure 3 shows an alignment for the trace $\langle A, B, D, C, E, E \rangle$ and the WF-net from Fig. 2. The first row of an alignment always corresponds to the given trace, ignoring the skip symbol $\gg$. The second row always corresponds to a valid firing sequence from the initial to the final marking. Each column represents a move; we distinguish four types: **synchronous moves** indicate a synchronization between the model and the trace, log moves indicate a *deviation*, i.e., the current activity in the trace is not replayed in the model, visible model moves indicate a *deviation*, i.e., the model executes an activity not observed in the trace at this stage, and invisible model moves indicate *no* real deviation, i.e., a model move on a transition labeled with τ. An alignment is *optimal* if it minimizes log moves and visible model moves. Note that multiple optimal alignments may exist for a given trace and a WF-net.

3   Model-Based Performance Analysis

This section introduces the model-based performance analysis approach in Cortado. The remainder is structured as follows. Section 3.1 introduces various performance indicators. Section 3.2 presents the implementation in Cortado from a user's perspective. Finally, Sect. 3.3 outlines the calculation and discusses open challenges.

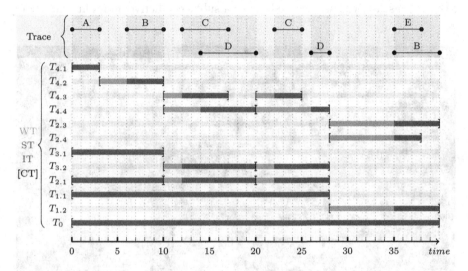

Fig. 4. Example of the PIs cycle (CT), service (ST), waiting (WT), and idle time (IT) based on a *fitting* trace for process tree T_0 (cf. Fig. 1). (Color figure online)

3.1   Defining Performance Indicators

Figure 4 depicts an example of the PIs computed by Cortado: waiting time (WT), service time (ST), idle time (IT), and cycle time (CT). The PIs are calculated for a given trace and process tree T_0 (cf. Fig. 1). At the top of Fig. 4, we show the trace, consisting of eight activities visualized as intervals. Below, we show the PIs for each subtree. For instance, the first row describes $T_{4.1}$. The [symbol indicates that $T_{4.1}$ was started at time 0 and the symbol] indicates its completion at time 3. After executing $T_{4.1}$, $T_{4.2}$ must be executed according to the process model, cf. Fig. 1. Thus, $T_{4.2}$ is enabled directly after the completion of $T_{4.1}$ at time 3. Since the activity B starts at time 6 according to the given trace, the waiting time of $T_{4.2}$ is 3. The leaf nodes $T_{4.1}$ and $T_{4.2}$ belong both to the subtree $T_{3.1}$. Thus, the cycle time of $T_{3.1}$ is 10, from the start of activity A at time 0 to the end of activity B at time 10. The service time of $T_{3.1}$ is 7, i.e., the union of the service times of its leaf nodes. The waiting time of $T_{3.1}$ is 0 because after the activation of $T_{3.1}$ at time 0, the activity A was directly executed. Finally, the idle time of $T_{3.1}$ is 3, which corresponds to the waiting time of $T_{4.2}$.

The idle time of leaf nodes is always zero because an activity cannot be paused since we only consider the start and completion of individual activities. The waiting time of an inner node corresponds to the time that elapses from its activation to the activation of its first executed leaf node. Note that the root node's waiting time is always zero since it is immediately activated when the first activity from the trace is executed. The root node is immediately closed when the last activity is executed. Once a subtree is active and a first leaf node

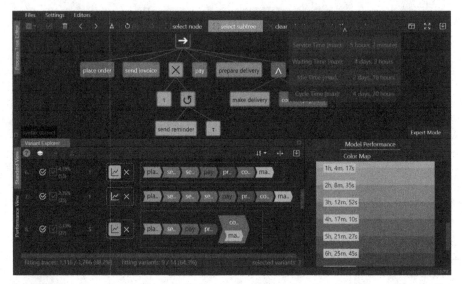

(a) Mapping max service times onto the process tree using traces corresponding to the selected variants 6., 7., and 8.

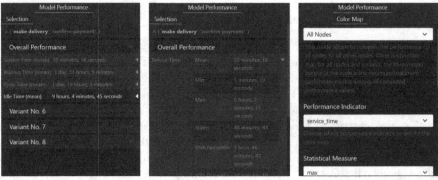

(b) PIs for the selected sub-tree per variant and overall.   (c) Selected subtree's service time for all variants.   (d) Color map settings.

Fig. 5. Example of the model-based performance functionality in Cortado

of this subtree has already been executed, periods in which no leaf node of the subtree is being executed are considered idle time. The execution of invisible leaf nodes happens instantly and does not cause any waiting, service, or idle time. For example, between closing $T_{3.1}$ and opening $T_{3.2}$ at time 10 (cf. Fig. 4) the invisible leaf node $T_{2.2}$ is executed (cf. Fig. 1). However, this execution is not visualized in Fig. 4 as it is irrelevant for the PIs. Finally, the cycle time of any (sub-)tree is the sum of its waiting, service, and idle times.

3.2 Realization in Cortado

We refer to [11] for a general introduction to the tool and details on Cortado's architecture. Cortado is available as a standalone build and can be downloaded from https://cortado.fit.fraunhofer.de. Figure 5 shows screenshots of the model-based performance analysis functionality. Figure 5a shows the entire User Interface (UI). The trace variants from the event log are visualized in the lower left UI-component, called the variant explorer. All shown variants in Fig. 5a are fitting the process tree, which is indicated by the green check-mark to the left of each variant. Variants 6, 7, and 8 are used for the model-based performance analysis because their performance analysis button is non-gray. As such, a user can individually select variants, i.e., traces corresponding to the variants, that should be used for performance analysis by pressing the performance analysis button. In the lower right UI-component (cf. Fig. 5a), a color map is displayed that currently shows the max service times in the tree. Note the subtree selected by the user highlighted in red (cf. Fig. 5a). The same UI-component displaying the color map (cf. Fig. 5a) also provides performance statistics for the selected subtree (cf. Fig. 5b). Cortado provides the PIs for this subtree either per variant or for all selected variants, i.e., overall performance (cf. Fig. 5). Figure 5c shows the service time statistics for the overall performance (all incorporated variants, i.e., 6, 7, and 8) for the selected subtree. As shown in Fig. 5d, the color map can be fully configured; all four PIs can be shown. Further, Cortado offers a second mode called *Variant Comparison* next to mode *All Nodes* (Fig. 5d), currently selected. The *Variant Comparison* mode allows comparing the performance of a variant to all other variants. Therefore, a user must select a single variant in the variant explorer by clicking on the performance button. The color map then shows how the performance of the selected variant compares to all other variants.

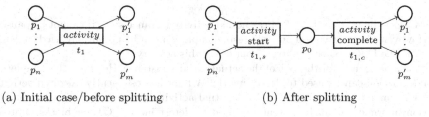

(a) Initial case/before splitting   (b) After splitting

Fig. 6. WF-net preparation for performance analysis—splitting visible transitions

3.3 Calculating PIs and Dealing with Non-fitting Traces

This section briefly outlines the computation of the presented PIs. First, we convert a given process tree into a WF net, as exemplified in Fig. 2. Next, we split each non-silent transition, which represent a process activity, into two transitions indicating the start and the completion of the related activity. Figure 6 illustrates this splitting. A non-silent transition t_1 labeled *activity* is split into two transitions $t_{1,1}$, representing the start of *activity*, and $t_{1,2}$, representing its completion. Next, we calculate an optimal alignment [2] for each trace using the prepared WF-net. Since the alignment provides a full execution sequence throughout the model, we can replay the trace and track the transitions' execution timestamps.

In general, the reliability of model-based performance analysis depends on the quality of the used process model, i.e., how accurately it represents reality [1, Section 3.3.3]. Thus, the significance of performance analysis is low if the event log and a model have little behavior in common. However, non-fitting traces, i.e., traces not entirely replayable on a process model, can be incorporated for performance analysis, cf. [2]. Also, Cortado allows the utilization of non-fitting traces for performance analysis.

Table 2 provides an overview of different situations, i.e., combinations of alignment moves for a single activity instance, and the corresponding possibilities regarding their incorporation into the calculation of PIs. For instance,

Table 2. Overview of calculable PIs for a process tree per alignment combination representing the start and completion of an activity

#	Alignment move combinations	Interpretation	WT	ST	IT	CT
1	Synchronous move on start & complete	Perfect activity instance	✓	✓	✓	✓
2	Synchronous move on start & model move on complete	Partial start	✓	–	✓[a]	–
3	Model move on start & synchronous move on complete	Partial complete	✓[b]	–	✓[a]	✓[c]
4	Model move on start & complete	Missing activity instance as per model	–	–	–	–
5	Log move	Missing activity instance as per log	–	–	–	–

[a] Cannot be used for the IT of the actual activity instance since it cannot be paused. However, the information on start resp. completion can be potentially used to determine the IT for blocks/subtrees containing this activity.

[b] Cannot be used for the WT of the actual activity instance. However, the completion information can be used to determine the WT for a subsequently executed activity.

[c] Cannot be used for the CT of the actual activity instance. Instead, the completion information can be potentially used to determine the CT for blocks/subtrees containing this activity.

the first alignment move combination is a synchronous move on an activity's start and completion. This combination is called a perfect activity instance, i.e., we could replay the start and the completion of an activity in the model as it occurred in the event data. Reconsider the example in Fig. 4 where each activity from the trace corresponds to a perfect activity instance. We can utilize the information from a perfect activity instance for all four indicators. In the second combination, we only know when an activity started, i.e., a synchronous move on the activity's start. However, we do not know precisely when it was completed as we observe a model move on complete. In this case, we can utilize the timing information from the synchronous move to calculate waiting times and cycle times of corresponding blocks and the entire process model. The third case describes a partial complete. This case is particularly interesting because many event logs do not contain two timestamps for each process activity in practice. Instead, only completion timestamps are available. Under these circumstances, we can still compute waiting, idle, and cycle times, cf. Table 2. Finally, we cannot use the alignment information for any PI calculation in the fourth and fifth cases.

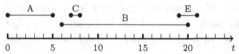

⟨A start, A complete, B start, C start, C complete, E start, B complete, E complete⟩

(a) Non-fitting trace and its sequential representation, used for alignment calculation

A start	A complete	B start	C start	≫	≫	C complete	E start	B complete	E complete
A start	A complete	B start	≫	B complete	B start	≫	E start	B complete	E complete
$t_{5,s}$	$t_{5,c}$	$t_{7,s}$		$t_{7,s}$	$t_{18,s}$		$t_{19,s}$	$t_{18,c}$	$t_{19,c}$
0	5	6	-	-	-	-	19	20	21

Service time of the root node: $ST(T_0) = (5-0) + (21-19) = 7$

A start	A complete	B start	≫	≫	C start	≫	C complete	≫	E start	B complete	E complete
A start	A complete	B start	B complete	D start	C start	D complete	C complete	B start	E start	B complete	E complete
$t_{5,s}$	$t_{5,c}$	$t_{7,s}$	$t_{7,s}$	$t_{10,s}$	$t_{9,s}$	$t_{10,c}$	$t_{9,c}$	$t_{18,s}$	$t_{19,s}$	$t_{18,c}$	$t_{19,c}$
0	5	6	-	-	7	-	8	19	-	21	

Service time of the root node: $ST(T_0) = (5-0) + (8-7) + (21-19) = 8$

A start	A complete	≫	≫	B start	C start	C complete	E start	B complete	E complete
A start	A complete	B start	B complete	B start	≫	≫	E start	B complete	E complete
$t_{5,s}$	$t_{5,c}$	$t_{7,s}$	$t_{7,s}$	$t_{18,s}$			$t_{19,s}$	$t_{18,c}$	$t_{19,c}$
0	5	-	-	6	-	-	19	20	21

Service time of the root node: $ST(T_0) = (5-0) + (21-6) = 20$

(b) Optimal alignments for the given trace and the WF-net from Fig. 2 after preparation (cf. Fig. 6). For simplicity, invisible model moves are omitted. Below each synchronous move, we show the respective timestamp. Perfect instances (cf. Table 2) are colored.

Fig. 7. Example of a non-fitting trace that causes unreliable performance analysis results, e.g., the service time of T_0 depends on which optimal alignment is used

Although non-fitting traces can be incorporated for performance analysis (cf. Table 2), the nature of alignments—multiple optimal alignments may exist for a given trace and model—adds a randomness factor to the performance analysis. A detailed examination of this problem is outside this paper's scope; instead, Fig. 7 illustrates an example of the problem. Figure 7b shows different optimal alignments for a trace (cf. Fig. 7a) and the WF-net from Fig. 2 after splitting transitions (cf. Fig. 6). Using these different alignments to compute the service time of the process tree root, i.e., $ST(T_0)$, we end up with three different values because each alignment finds different perfect activity instances (cf. Table 2). Since only perfect activity instances can be used for service time calculation (cf. Table 2), the service time depends on the optimal alignment found. Cortado, therefore, warns the user if non-fitting traces are used for performance analysis.

4   Related Work and Tools

This section provides a brief overview of related work and tools to highlight the differences in the proposed approach. Note that an extensive and complete overview is outside this paper's scope. The fundamental idea of analyzing the temporal performance of a process and enriching process models with performance statistics has been discussed in [1, Chapter 9], [6, Chapter 7], and [4, Chapter 10]. In [2, Chapter 9], the author describes how alignments can be utilized for performance analysis for Petri nets. The usage of alignments for the performance analysis of YAWL models has been shown in [3].

We surveyed commercial and academic tools: ABBYY Timeline, Apromore [7], ARIS Process Mining, Celonis, Disco, IBM Process Mining, Minit, and the ProM [5] plugins: Inductive Visual Miner [9], Replay Log in YAWL net [10], Discover using the Statechart Workbench [8], and Replay a Log on Petri Net for Performance Analysis [2]. All commercial tools and the Inductive Visual Miner provide performance analysis for Directly-Follows-Graphs (DFG). A DFG is a directed graph representing the directly follows relation of process activities. The expressiveness of a DFG is, however, limited [12] compared to the expressiveness of, e.g., process trees. Performance analysis for non-DFG models is only supported by Apromore, ARIS, and the ProM plugins. The plugin Discover using the Statechart Workbench [8] also supports hierarchical performance analysis of process trees as Cortado, but it only offers cycle time statistics per block. In contrast, Cortado's approach calculates various PIs for each block.

5   Conclusion

This paper presented the performance analysis functionality of Cortado. Focusing on block-structured models, PIs—we presented cycle, idle, waiting, and service time—can be calculated for each block, each of which represents a part of the overall process model. The main challenges for future work remain the scalability of the alignment computation and the highlighted problem of incorporating non-fitting traces in model-based performance analysis.

References

1. van der Aalst, W.M.P.: Process Mining. Springer, Heidelberg (2016). https://doi. org/10.1007/978-3-662-49851-4
2. Adriansyah, A.: Aligning observed and modeled behavior. Ph.D. thesis (2014). https://doi.org/10.6100/IR770080
3. Adriansyah, A., Van Dongen, B., Piessens, D., Wynn, M., Adams, M.: Robust performance analysis on yawl process models with advanced constructs. J. Inf. Technol. Theor. Appl. (JITTA) **12**(3) (2012). https://doi.org/10.1.1.227.6079
4. Carmona, J., van Dongen, B.F., Solti, A., Weidlich, M.: Conformance Checking - Relating Processes and Models. Springer, Cham (2018). https://doi.org/10.1007/ 978-3-319-99414-7
5. van Dongen, B.F., de Medeiros, A.K.A., Verbeek, H.M.W., Weijters, A.J.M.M., van der Aalst, W.M.P.: The ProM framework: a new era in process mining tool support. In: Ciardo, G., Darondeau, P. (eds.) ICATPN 2005. LNCS, vol. 3536, pp. 444–454. Springer, Heidelberg (2005). https://doi.org/10.1007/11494744_25
6. Dumas, M., Rosa, M.L., Mendling, J., Reijers, H.A.: Fundamentals of Business Process Management. Springer, Heidelberg (2013). https://doi.org/10.1007/978-3-642-33143-5
7. La Rosa, M., et al.: APROMORE: an advanced process model repository. Exp. Syst. Appl. **38**(6) (2011). https://doi.org/10.1016/j.eswa.2010.12.012
8. Leemans, M., van der Aalst, W.M.P., van den Brand, M.G.J.: Hierarchical performance analysis for process mining. Association for Computing Machinery (2018). https://doi.org/10.1145/3202710.3203151
9. Leemans, S.J.J.(ed.): Robust Process Mining with Guarantees. LNBIP, vol. 440. Springer, Cham (2022). https://doi.org/10.1007/978-3-030-96655-3
10. Piessens, D., Wynn, M.T., Adams, M., van Dongen, B.F., et al.: Performance analysis of business process models with advanced constructs (2010)
11. Schuster, D., van Zelst, S.J., van der Aalst, W.M.P.: Cortado—an interactive tool for data-driven process discovery and modeling. In: Buchs, D., Carmona, J. (eds.) PETRI NETS 2021. LNCS, vol. 12734, pp. 465–475. Springer, Cham (2021). https://doi.org/10.1007/978-3-030-76983-3_23
12. van der Aalst, W.M.P.: A practitioner's guide to process mining: limitations of the directly-follows graph. Procedia Comput. Sci. **164** (2019). https://doi.org/10. 1016/j.procs.2019.12.189

Generating Purpose-Driven Explanations: The Case of Process Predictive Model Inspection

Bemali Wickramanayake, Chun Ouyang$^{(\boxtimes)}$ (ID), Catarina Moreira (ID), and Yue Xu (ID)

Queensland University of Technology, Brisbane, QLD 4000, Australia
{kota.wickramanayake,c.ouyang,catarina.pintomoreira,yue.xu}@qut.edu.au

Abstract. Explainable AI is an emerging branch of data science that focuses on demystifying the complex computation logic of machine learning with an aim to improve the transparency, validity and trust in automated decisions. While existing research focuses on building methods and techniques to explain 'black-box' models, much attention has not been paid to generating model explanations. Effective model explanations are often driven by the purpose of explanation in a given problem context. In this paper, we propose a framework to support generating model explanations for the purpose of model inspection in the context of predictive process analytics. We build a visual explanation platform as an implementation of the proposed framework for inspecting and analysing a process predictive model, and demonstrate the applicability of the framework using a real-life case study on a loan application process.

Keywords: Explainable AI · Explanation purpose ·
Model inspection · predictive process analytics · Visualisation

1 Introduction

The modern world has been evolving rapidly with the advent of many cutting-edge technologies. An example of such advancement is automated decision making underpinned by machine learning capabilities. However, concerns about the validity and fairness of the decision making process of machine learning models (which broadly include deep learning models) have also been raised. Explainable AI (XAI) is an emerging area that aims to fill the gap between automated decision making and human understanding, especially in high-stake decision making [9].

A model explanation is closely associated with two key elements—the purpose of explanation and problem context. For an instance, we consider the two research efforts [11,13] concerning different purposes and problem contexts. In [11], the authors use model explanations to achieve an accurate and explainable detection of a brain disease using medical images as input. In [13], the

J. De Weerdt and A. Polyvyanyy (Eds.): CAiSE Forum 2022, LNBIP 452, pp. 120–129, 2022.
https://doi.org/10.1007/978-3-031-07481-3_14

authors aim to improve a given business process using explanations of a predictive model trained to predict future status of that process. However, due to the lack of a systematic method or framework to guide the design, existing approaches for extracting explanations from a 'black-box model' are often developed in an ad-hoc manner, despite the existence of a specific purpose in a given problem context.

Our research is inspired by the idea that effective model explanations are often driven by the purpose of explanation in a given problem context. As per a stakeholder survey, one of the top three purposes of demystifying a model is inspecting and debugging the model itself [2]. In this paper, we are interested in inspecting models trained for making process predictions, and hence we propose a framework to support generating model explanations for the purpose of model inspection in the context of predictive process analytics. We build a visual explanation platform as an implementation of the proposed framework for inspecting and analysing a process predictive model, and demonstrate the applicability of the framework using a real-life case study on a loan application process with a Dutch financial institution.

2 Background and Related Work

2.1 Model Explanations

Whilst the primary objective of explainable AI is opening 'black-box' models to provide transparency, There are nine different end purposes, informed by the exact motivation behind generating model explanations [14]. Inspection (or debugging) is among these nine purposes, which allows users to identify defects in a model or system.

Model explanations can be extracted at various stages of model development [7]. This can be classified as *pre-model explanations*, which refer to exploratory data analysis that is carried out prior to developing the model, and *in-model and post-model explanations*, which refer to explanation of model decision logic that could be extracted by using either the interpretable model itself (in-model) or post-hoc methods (post-model) [3].

Explanations are presented at the granularity of either *local* (single sample), *global* (the entire model) or *cohort* level (subset of the sample space) to address the purpose of model explanation [4,15].

Model explanations are important to address humans need of understanding phenomena of intrigue [19]. They can take various forms which include *feature importance*, *component data* (data points with model outcome), *model internals* (algorithmic representations), *explanation by case*, *contrastive*, *counterfactual*, *evidence* (information that supports a diagnosis), *prediction certainty*, *input data*, and *system performance* [17].

2.2 Explainable Predictive Process Analytics

Predictive process analytics is an emerging sub domain in the area of process mining, which is underpinned by machine learning techniques. It aims to build the capability for predicting a future status of an ongoing process trace. Most commonly, process predictive models are developed to predict the *outcome*, *next event* or *remaining execution time* of a process trace to meet a specific organization goal, such as process control and improvement.

Model explainability is gaining increasing attention in predictive process analytics. Amongst the post-hoc approaches of explaining process predictive models, we can observe the use of SHAP [8], LIME [16], surrogate decision trees [12] and partial dependence plots [13]. Attention weights [18] and Layer-wise Relevance Propagation [20] have been used as intrinsic techniques for explaining deep learning-based process predictions.

However, we can observe only few among the existing studies that generate model explanations for a specific purpose, such as the work of [12,13] for process improvement and the work of [16] for model improvement.

3 Framework

We propose a framework to guide generating explanations for the purpose of inspecting process predictive models (see Fig. 1). The framework consists of four layers capturing model development life cycle, explanation extraction, consolidation, and presentation, respectively; and two pillars capturing the sequence of tasks for model inspection (the right pillar) and the problem context of predictive process analytics (the left pillar).

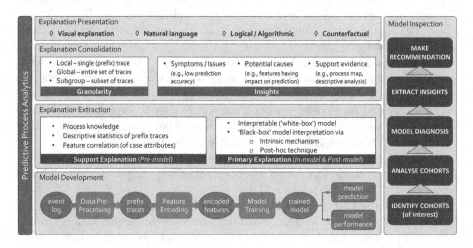

Fig. 1. Framework for generating purpose-driven explanations in the case of process predictive model inspection

3.1 Model Development

At each phase of the machine learning model development life cycle [22], there are information elements that can be extracted [7] to explain the model. A process predictive model development involves exploration of input event logs, converting event log data into meaningful features using various encoding techniques, and training the process predictive model.

3.2   Explanation Extraction

This layer represents the extraction of model explanations at various stages of model development. We define two levels of model explanations as follows.

- *Primary explanations* describe how the model makes decisions. If the model is not a white-box (such as a decision tree or a linear regression model), intrinsic and post-hoc mechanisms can be used to explain the model [9]. With the primary explanations, we can identify which features or data points have influenced the model decision.
- *Support explanations* refer to the information that would help to identify potential problems with the aspects of a model to inspect (e.g., model performance and predictions), and supports the primary explanations by providing further evidence (e.g., descriptive statistics of the prefix traces, process domain knowledge, notes and annotations).

3.3   Explanation Consolidation and Presentation

The next two layers focus on generating meaningful explanations through information consolidation (explanation consolidation) and presenting and communicating the explanations to users (explanation presentation), respectively.

- *Explanation granularity* refers to the level of granularity [4,15] at which explanations will be analysed. The three key levels of explanation granularity are: *local* for explanation of a single instance, *subset/cohort* level for explanation of a subset of instances, and *global* for explanation of an entire model. In the case of model inspection, the issues with predictions are identified using global and/or cohort level explanations [15]. These can be further validated with local explanations by analysing how the prediction was made for an individual prefix trace.
- *Insights* refer to meaningful information derived from the abstract explanations. We classify them into three categories; *symptoms* which indicate an issue in the model, *potential causes* which suggest a possible reason for those symptoms, and *support evidences* that further validate those reasons. For the purpose of model inspection, often poor predictive performance is seen as a typical symptom. Potential causes for poor performance are identified by examining primary explanations [5,16]. Identified causes can be further validated with the support evidences that may include process knowledge and descriptive statistics of prefix-traces.
- *Presentation of insights* can be supported using an appropriate technique such as visual, natural language based, algorithmic, and counterfactual [6]. The exact technique to be chosen depends on the nature of insights and target audience.

3.4   Model Inspection

We are interested in inspecting an under-performing process predictive model. The recent work that focus on inspecting and debugging machine learning models using model explanations follow a systematic approach. The approach mainly involves partitioning the model into sub cohorts, isolating the problematic predictions, identifying the causes behind such predictions using model explanations [10], correcting these issues using an appropriate strategy such as removal of faulty features or data points, and re-training the model. Hence, we propose five steps for systematically inspecting a model using model explanations.

(1) Specify model cohorts (model partitioning based on inputs)
(2) Identify problematic cohorts that display poor predictive performance
(3) Use primary model explanations to identify which features or properties of the inputs result in such poor performance and arrive at a primary diagnosis that is specific to the cohort
(4) Strengthen the primary diagnosis with support explanations
(5) Recommendation for fixing the identified issue

4   Case Study

For demonstration of the proposed framework, we have implemented a visual analytics platform for model inspection guided by our framework. For demonstration of the framework we use a LSTM-based deep learning model [21] which predicts next activity for a given process prefix trace with a publicly available real-life event log [1]. The link to the interactive model explanation can be found at: https://tinyurl.com/Visualexplanation4inspection.

4.1   Process Predictive Model and Model Explanations

As the primary explanation technique, we use attention weights from the LSTM architecture to obtain feature importance. This is an intrinsic (in-model) explanation technique. To support the primary explanations, we obtain pre-model explanations that describe the properties and relationships in the underlying dataset and the process model of the underlying process (using an existing process discovery tool) as a representation of process domain knowledge.

4.2   Visual Explanations for Model Inspection

A visual model explanation is developed on Microsoft Power BI data visualisation platform. The design is customized for the purpose of model inspection in the context of predictive process analytics. This implementation (see Fig. 2) can be adapted for any process predictive model using standard event logs as input.

Frame 1 of Fig. 2 dissects the model into cohorts via the dimensions of (a) Process Decision Point, (b) Prediction Target and (c) Model Performance. Subframes 1.1 and 1.2 depict the model recall by the prediction target and model precision by the actual prediction, respectively. With the top right filter, process decision point at which the prediction was made can be selected. Sub-frames 1.3 and 1.4 show the number of predictions that fall in each sub category, which helps to quantify the magnitude of the cohort.

Frame 2 of Fig. 2 contains the model explanations for the cohort of interest identified at Frame 1 (using the selection panel at top). Sub-frame 2.3 is the primary explanation by feature importance for the selected cohort. Local (instance level) feature importance is aggregated at the cohort level in terms of average

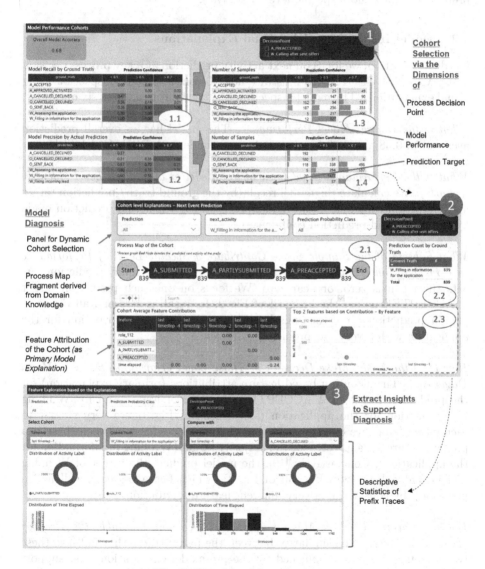

Fig. 2. Visual model explanations

feature weight and top two feature values voted by the majority of the cohort. To assist with the primary explanation, the fragment of the process map for the selected cohort indicates key paths of the process map leading to the prediction (sub-frame 2.1). Sub-frame 2.2 is a breakdown of the prediction count for a given prediction, by prediction target which helps analysing misclassification.

Frame 3 of Fig. 2 is designed to support any conclusions arrived at Frame 2, with the statistical properties of prefix traces contained in the selected cohort. It has an additional filter where the user can select the exact time step of the prefix trace, for a more specific level of analysis.

4.3   Model Inspection with Visual Explanations

For demonstration, we focus on next activity prediction at a key process decision point A_PREACCEPTED to illustrate how to conduct model inspection using visual explanations. The model inspection is carried out to address six questions.

What is the Overall Model Performance: The model has an overall prediction accuracy of 0.68 and 0.70 for the predictions made at A_PREACCEPTED.

What is the Performance Breakdown of the Model at the Subset Level (Identify Cohorts): We calculate the model recall (by the ground truth/ prediction target and prediction confidence) and model precision (by the actual prediction made by the model and prediction confidence).

What Subsets of the Sample Space Contribute a Specific Level of Performance in Consideration (Analyse Cohorts): We observe that for many prediction targets the recall is zero, or near zero. We focus on one such prediction target A_ACCEPTED as per the Frame 1 of Fig. 2. Its recall is zero and all the samples in prediction target are misclassified as W_filling in information for the application with a very low prediction confidence.

How Does the Model Make Decision in Those Low Performance Subsets (Model Diagnosis): The attention based feature attributions (primary explanation) for the prediction target of A_ACCEPTED (frame 2 of Fig. 2) and for W_filling in information for the application (sub Fig. 3a of Fig. 3) are very similar to each other. Thus, we can conclude that the model confuses between these two prediction targets, and votes for the majority target (W_filling in information for the application). Contrastively [10], the model predicts the target of W_fixing and incoming lead (Sub Fig. 3b of Fig. 3) (which has a perfect recall and a precision), by considering a very different feature attribution.

Do the Features Used in Making the Model Decision Resemble the Reality? (Extract Insights): The similarity between the prefix traces that fall into these two targets are further confirmed by the pre-model explanations, i.e. support evidences based on prefix trace analysis (frame 3 of Fig. 2).

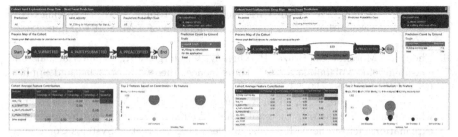

| (a) W_filling in information | (b) W_fixing and incoming lead |

Fig. 3. Contrastive explanations

Recommendation: Information considered in the original feature space ('activity label', 'resource label' and 'time elapsed') are not sufficient to predict certain targets accurately, especially early on the process.

5 Conclusion and Future Work

We have proposed a framework to render model explanations for the purpose of model inspection in the context of predictive process analytics. The framework guides the visual implementation of model explanation, and effectively supports the model inspection by identifying the low performing cohorts, and the reason behind such poor predictive performance. As future work, we expect to conduct a model inspection task, using model explanations, which will then help generate recommendations for model improvement. We expect to enhance generation of model explanations by engaging potential user cohorts (data scientists). We also plan to extend the framework for a different purpose.

Acknowledgments. The reported research is part of a PhD project supported by a Science and Engineering Faculty scholarship and a Centre for Data Science top up scholarship at Queensland University of Technology (QUT). It also received funding support from Centre for Data Science First Byte Funding Program at QUT as well as QUT's Women in Research Grant Scheme.

References

1. BPI Challenge 2012: Event log of a loan application process (2012)
2. Brennen, A.: What do people really want when they say they want "Explainable AI?" We asked 60 stakeholders. In: CHI Conference on Human Factors in Computing Systems Extended Abstracts. ACM, April 2020
3. Carvalho, D.V., Pereira, E.M., Cardoso, J.S.: Machine learning interpretability: a survey on methods and metrics. Electronics **8**(8), 832 (2019)
4. Chan, G.Y., Bertini, E., Nonato, L.G., Barr, B., Silva, C.T.: Melody: generating and visualizing machine learning model summary to understand data and classifiers together. CoRR abs/2007.10614 (2020)

5. Chen, C.J., Chen, L.W., Yang, C.H., Huang, Y.Y., Huang, Y.M.: Improving CNN-based pest recognition with a post-hoc explanation of XAI. Soft Comput. (2021, in Review)

6. Chou, Y., Moreira, C., Bruza, P., Ouyang, C., Jorge, J.A.: Counterfactuals and causability in explainable artificial intelligence: theory, algorithms, and applications. Inf. Fusion **81**, 59–83 (2022)

7. Dhanorkar, S., Wolf, C.T., Qian, K., Xu, A., Popa, L., Li, Y.: Who needs to know what, when?: Broadening the explainable AI (XAI) design space by looking at explanations across the AI lifecycle. In: Designing Interactive Systems Conference. ACM, June 2021

8. Galanti, R., Coma-Puig, B., de Leoni, M., Carmona, J., Navarin, N.: Explainable predictive process monitoring. In: 2020 2nd International Conference on Process Mining (ICPM). IEEE, October 2020

9. Guidotti, R., Monreale, A., Ruggieri, S., Turini, F., Giannotti, F., Pedreschi, D.: A survey of methods for explaining black box models. ACM Comput. Surv. **51**(5), 1–42 (2019)

10. Krishnan, S., Wu, E.: Palm: machine learning explanations for iterative debugging. In: Proceedings of the 2nd Workshop on Human-In-the-Loop Data Analytics, HILDA 2017. Association for Computing Machinery, New York (2017)

11. Lee, H., et al.: An explainable deep-learning algorithm for the detection of acute intracranial haemorrhage from small datasets. Nat. Biomed. Eng. **3**(3), 173–182 (2018)

12. Mehdiyev, N., Fettke, P.: Prescriptive process analytics with deep learning and explainable artificial intelligence. In: 28th European Conference on Information Systems. An Online AIS Conference (2020)

13. Mehdiyev, N., Fettke, P.: Explainable artificial intelligence for process mining: a general overview and application of a novel local explanation approach for predictive process monitoring. In: Pedrycz, W., Chen, S.-M. (eds.) Interpretable Artificial Intelligence: A Perspective of Granular Computing. SCI, vol. 937, pp. 1–28. Springer, Cham (2021). https://doi.org/10.1007/978-3-030-64949-4_1

14. Nunes, I., Jannach, D.: A systematic review and taxonomy of explanations in decision support and recommender systems. User Model. User-Adap. Inter. **27**(3–5), 393–444 (2017)

15. Ribera, M., Lapedriza, À.: Can we do better explanations? A proposal of user-centered explainable AI. In: IUI Workshops (2019)

16. Rizzi, W., Di Francescomarino, C., Maggi, F.M.: Explainability in predictive process monitoring: when understanding helps improving. In: Fahland, D., Ghidini, C., Becker, J., Dumas, M. (eds.) BPM 2020. LNBIP, vol. 392, pp. 141–158. Springer, Cham (2020). https://doi.org/10.1007/978-3-030-58638-6_9

17. Schoonderwoerd, T.A., Jorritsma, W., Neerincx, M.A., van den Bosch, K.: Human-centered XAI: developing design patterns for explanations of clinical decision support systems. Int. J. Hum. Comput. Stud. **154**, 102684 (2021)

18. Sindhgatta, R., Moreira, C., Ouyang, C., Barros, A.: Exploring interpretable predictive models for business processes. In: Fahland, D., Ghidini, C., Becker, J., Dumas, M. (eds.) BPM 2020. LNCS, vol. 12168, pp. 257–272. Springer, Cham (2020). https://doi.org/10.1007/978-3-030-58666-9_15

19. Wang, D., Yang, Q., Abdul, A., Lim, B.Y.: Designing theory-driven user-centric explainable AI. In: Proceedings of the 2019 CHI Conference on Human Factors in Computing Systems. ACM, May 2019

20. Weinzierl, S., Zilker, S., Brunk, J., Revoredo, K., Matzner, M., Becker, J.: XNAP: making LSTM-based next activity predictions explainable by using LRP. In: Del Río Ortega, A., Leopold, H., Santoro, F.M. (eds.) BPM 2020. LNBIP, vol. 397, pp. 129–141. Springer, Cham (2020). https://doi.org/10.1007/978-3-030-66498-5_10
21. Wickramanayake, B., He, Z., Ouyang, C., Moreira, C., Xu, Y., Sindhgatta, R.: Building interpretable models for business process prediction using shared and specialised attention mechanisms. Knowl. Based Syst. (2022, in Press)
22. Wirth, R., Hipp, J.: CRISP-DM: towards a standard process model for data mining (2000)

Generating Synthetic Sensor Event Logs
for Process Mining

Yorck Zisgen$^{(\boxtimes)}$, Dominik Janssen, and Agnes Koschmider

Group Process Analytics, Kiel University, Kiel, Germany
{yzi,dominik.janssen,ak}@informatik.uni-kiel.de

Abstract. Process mining has gained significant practical usefulness in diverse domains. The input of process mining is an event log, tracking the execution of activities that can be mapped onto a business processes. Thus, the availability and quality of event logs significantly impact the process mining result. The use of process mining in novel use cases or experimental settings is often hampered because no appropriate event logs are available. This paper presents a tool to generate synthetic (sensor) event logs. Compared to existing synthetic log generator tools, the IoT process log generator produces data in a non-deterministic way. Users can add noise in a controlled manner and might enhance the processes with IoT data. In this way, the tool allows generating synthetic data for IoT environments that can be individually configured. Our tool makes a contribution towards an increased use of process mining in settings relying on (IoT) sensor event data.

Keywords: Internet of things · Event log simulation · Synthetic data · Business process simulation · Process mining

1 Introduction

Process Mining and Internet-of-Things (IoT) can significantly benefit from each other because IoT environments produce the large quantity of data that process mining methods require for accurate process analysis [11]. In turn, process mining provides the insights to understand the IoT enhanced processes in a controlled way. However, quality issues of the high volume of IoT data (like missing or incomplete data entries) hamper the direct applicability of process mining on IoT data. Additionally, sensor event data is at a much lower level of semantics, and the data does not directly relate to high-level business process concepts as required for process mining.

To allow working on IoT data of different data quality that can be used by process mining, this paper presents the *IoT process log generator*. The tool generates both synthetic event logs and synthetic IoT sensor event logs. For this purpose, a simulation engine with an end-user front end has been implemented. Users model processes and can configure the process models in terms of duration, frequency of process activities, or noise. Optionally they can specify an

J. De Weerdt and A. Polyvyanyy (Eds.): CAiSE Forum 2022, LNBIP 452, pp. 130–137, 2022.
https://doi.org/10.1007/978-3-031-07481-3_15

IoT environment that is mapped to the process model. In this way, event logs for varying IoT environments (with different sensor or failure types) can be produced and used for experimental purposes. For instance, motion sensors with discrete ON and OFF states or temperature sensors with continuous values can be configured. Also, a simulation can be used to answer questions of whether upgrading a facility with IoT sensors will justify the occurred cost. It can also help to reveal bottlenecks in production capacity by showing potential congestion in the simulation. Generally, it has been shown that synthetic data not only provide a substitution for real data [3,16], but can even enhance insight into domain-specific research [19]. Thus, we are convinced that our IoT process log generator will fuel the application of process mining in use cases where data accessibility is challenging and data quality also hampers data analysis.

This paper is structured as follows. Section 2 summarizes related works. Section 3 presents the general architecture of our tool, while Sect. 4 provides an in-depth look into the implementation. Section 5 demonstrates the applicability of our tool on two use cases. Finally, the paper concludes with a summary and a discussion of future tasks.

2   Related Work

The following streams of research are related to the IoT process log generator: (1) IoT log generators and (2) event log generators.

Generally, the available works are either limited to a certain sensor type [9, 15], are restricted to a particular application domain [2,15], or only provide a collection of IoT simulation approaches [1,4,18]. For instance, the approaches presented in [9,15] are limited to GPS or signal strength sensor types and do not allow to add additional sensor types. In contrast our IoT process log generator allows to add additional sensor types like motion, light, temperature, counter or on/off sensors in the analysis.

Diverse application domains have been tackled by IoT log generators like mobile devices, wireless sensor networks or cyberphysical systems. For instance, Kertesz et al. [13] propose a simulator for the cloud communication of mobile IoT devices' sensor data. Papadoupolos et al. [15] addressed signal strength of wireless sensor networks. Ramprasad et al. [17] propose a simulator for virtual IoT architectures called EMU-IoT, in which an end-to-end evaluation of an IoT network can be simulated. Gimênez et al. [9] tested changing positional data to test collision anticipation of vehicles in a warehouse. Ahmad et al. [2] proposed a simulation architecture to commit research on communication in real-time-IoT environments. Thus, available IoT simulators are commonly designed around a narrow application field. They do not allow for usage in more diverse settings like the IoT process log generator, which allows to run simulations such as visitor amount monitoring, smart home activities, procedures in a smart factory, or hospital processes.

Synthetic event logs might also be generated with the CPN tool [12], ProM [20] or WoPed [7], which are common tools for process modeling or process mining respectively. Also, a log generator for declarative process models has been suggested [5]. However, these tools only create deterministic event logs that directly result from the behavior of the modeled process (i.e., no frequency of trace occurrence can be specified). Furthermore, ProM allows to add noise and outliers into the event log. However, a recent analysis of these noise adding plug-ins showed that available noise filtering tools do not appropriately filter nor add noise [14]. In contrast, our IoT process log generator makes it possible to introduce different noise types, while still providing a corresponding noise-free log as ground truth for comparison.

To sum up, the available IoT log generators are restricted to specific sensor types or application domains, while our tool is not restricted to any specific sensor type or domain. It also generates data in a non-deterministic way, can add noise in a controlled way and it can be expanded to include other sensor or noise types.

3   Architecture

This section presents the architecture of the IoT process log generator. Figure 1 shows the architectural design. The tool is platform-independent, is designed for single-user settings, and was developed in Python version 3.9, using NumPy [10] as an external library. The tool can be accessed publicly via a browser. Users can model processes with Petri nets in the online modeler or import .PNML files. Additionally, they can manage simulation settings, such as duration of activities, simulated time range, and add different types and quantities of noise. They can use the IoT environment to configure an IoT environment (i.e., specify sensor types and failure probabilities). Subsequently, two different types of event logs can be generated at the application layer, either a *conventional* event log with time-stamps and activities or an IoT sensor event log with additional sensor information. The settings configuration and the designed IoT environment are used as input in a way that each process activity is mapped onto locations in the IoT environment. Finally, the information generated by the application layer is processed into an event log that can be read on-screen or downloaded as a

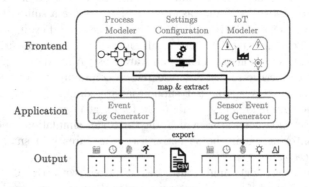

Fig. 1. Architecture of the IoT process log generator

.TXT- or .CSV-file. The next section explains in detail the conceptual design of the IoT process log generator.

4   Implementation

Figure 2 extends Fig. 1 and shows the information flow within our IoT process log generator. First, the modeled processes, the configuration settings and the desired output format are forwarded to the simulation engine (see **1**, **2**, **3**). The simulation engine creates process instances from the business process(es) (**4**). Those process instances (consisting of places and transitions) are processed independently of one another. Internally, they follow the execution rules of Petri nets (**5**, **6**). Transitions represent activities, which are mapped to locations in an IoT environment (**8**) and activate sensors (**7**). Movements within the environment (**9**) can also activate sensors (**10**). Sensor readings (continuous or discrete) then adhere to the IoT settings and finally transmit their information, timestamps, and optionally noise, to the sensor event log (**11**). If a user only aims for an event log, the IoT modeler is skipped and the event log is directly generated (**12**). Figure 3 shows the technical design of the IoT process log generator in terms of a UML class diagram.

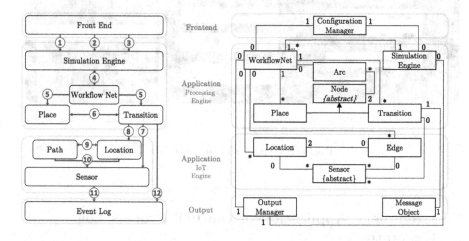

Fig. 2. Information flow   **Fig. 3.** UML class diagram extract

Our work distinguishes itself from a processing script by avoiding any deterministic proceedings when exclusive choices or parallel activities are modeled. Furthermore activity duration and sensor values are determined by choosing a random value within a given interval and a probability distribution. As a consequence, all possible execution sequences of a business process can be tracked in the event log. Activity duration is randomly set to a value within the range specified for this activity. Sensor activation can be set to happen at any time during the activation, in either a given or random order. Furthermore, we permit to specify probabilities for each choice to allow for a *'standard case execution'* and an *'outlier case execution'*.

Figure 4 shows exemplary the GUI of our tool. The user has modeled a Petri net referring to a hospital process (see Figs. 4a and 4b). The generator will simulate the modeled process ten times within a six-hour time frame. Noise with an occurrence rate of 50.7% is added to the output. According to the selection, the following types of noise will be included: dropping events, duplicating events (i.e., event twice), and assigning a wrong event value (Fig. 4c).

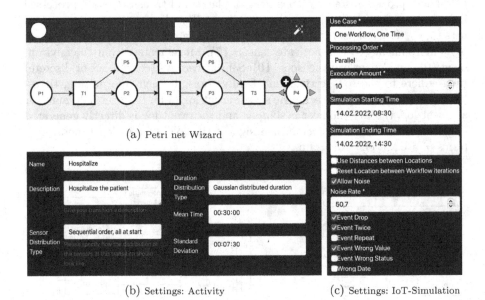

(a) Petri net Wizard

(b) Settings: Activity   (c) Settings: IoT-Simulation

Fig. 4. Screenshots of web interface

5   Exemplary Application of the IoT Process Log Generator

In this section, we demonstrate the usefulness of our tool using two examples: hospital processes and smart homes. To generate an event log for a hospital process, we took the process described in Elkoumy et al. [8]. We translated the BPMN process to a Petri net, configured the settings of the process (i.e., used different activity durations, added noise), and simulated the process. Based on the simulation and the user's configuration, an event log has been generated as shown in Table 1. The left-hand side of the table shows the clean event log (*ground truth*), while the right-hand side of the table includes noise according to the user specifications.

Table 1. Synthetic hospital event logs

Log - Clean			Log - Noise			
Case ID	Date Time	Activity	Case ID	Date Time	Activity	Noise Type
846	2022-02-24 08:23	Register	846	2022-02-24 20:23	Register	Wrong Time
846	2022-02-24 09:07	Hospitalize	846	2022-02-24 09:07	Hospitalize	Event Twice
			846	2022-02-24 09:07	Hospitalize	Event Twice
846	2022-02-24 10:46	Blood Test	846	2022-24-02 10:46	Blood Test	Wrong Date
846	2022-02-24 11:18	Blood Test				Event Lost
846	2022-02-24 12:18	Visit	846	2022-02-24 12:18	Visit	Multi Recordings
			846	2022-02-24 12:21	Visit	Multi Recordings
			846	2022-02-24 12:22	Visit	Multi Recordings
846	2022-02-24 13:12	Discharge	846	2022-02-24 13:12	Register	Wrong Event
(a) Event Log Clean			(b) Event Log with added Noise			

The second example is related to smart homes. For this purpose, we took a sensor event log from literature [6] observing activities of smart home inhabitants with various sensors. We designed an IoT environment with the IoT modeler, added different sensor types, and simulated daily routines like *cooking, cleaning up* or *making breakfast*. Additionally, we added noise to the configuration. Tables 2a and 2b show the results.

6   Summary and Future Work

This paper presented the IoT process log generator, a tool to generate synthetic (sensor) event logs. Our generator not only creates event logs usable as ground truth. Additionally, it offers to add an adjustable degree of erroneous entries (noise) to enable working on imperfect and, therefore, more realistic data. In this way, the synthetic event logs might be used to validate process discovery algorithms, increase the quality of event logs, and also pave the way for novel use cases based on (IoT) sensor event data.

Table 2. Synthetic sensor event logs

Log - Clean			Log - Noise			
Sensor ID	DateTime	Value	Sensor ID	DateTime	Value	Noise Type
S1	2022-03-04 08:13	Off	S1	2022-03-04 20:13	Off	Wrong Time
S2	2022-03-04 08:17	On	S2	2022-03-04 08:17	On	Event Twice
			S2	2022-03-04 08:17	On	Event Twice
S3	2022-03-04 08:25	Off				Event Lost
S4	2022-03-24 08:36	On	S4	2022-03-24 08:36	On	Multi Recordings
			S4	2022-03-24 08:36	On	Multi Recordings
			S4	2022-03-24 08:37	On	Multi Recordings
S5	2022-03-04 08:58	Off	S5	2022-04-03 08:58	Off	Wrong Date
F26	2022-03-04 09:33	96.22	S2	2022-03-04 09:33	On	Wrong Sensor
S6	2022-03-04 09:42	On	S6	2022-03-04 09:42	Off	Wrong Status
F27	2022-03-04 09:56	0.493	F27	2022-03-04 09:56	0.557	Wrong Value
(a) Sensor Event Log Clean			(b) Sensor Event Log with added Noise			

As for now, our generator is capable of generating event logs for single-user settings. We plan to extend the IoT modeler with a multi-agent capability and role-based task simulation. This extension will enable the assignment of resources and individual availabilities to specific process activities. In future iterations, we will allow more process modeling notations, increase the number of output formats, and enhance the process visualization. The upcoming versions will include BPMN 2.0 as an alternative input format. We plan to use random seeds for the non-deterministic parts of the generator to ensure the reproducibility of experiments. Beside .CSV and .TXT as output formats, it is planned to output the event logs as .XES-files. To enhance the visualization of the process models, we plan to include a 3D modeler allowing to visually create a realistic 3D environment and to augment the process model. A corresponding 3D plug-in has been already presented [21].

References

1. Ahmad, S., Malik, S., Kim, D.H.: Comparative analysis of simulation tools with visualization based on realtime task scheduling algorithms for IoT embedded applications. Int. J. Grid Distrib. Comput. **11**, 1–10 (2018). https://doi.org/10.14257/ijgdc.2018.11.2.01

2. Ahmad, S., Malik, S., Ullah, I., Park, D.H., Kim, K., Kim, D.: Towards the design of a formal verification and evaluation tool of real-time tasks scheduling of IoT applications. Sustainability **11**(1), 204 (2019). https://doi.org/10.3390/su11010204

3. Chen, J., Chun, D., Patel, M., Chiang, E., James, J.: The validity of synthetic clinical data: a validation study of a leading synthetic data generator (Synthea) using clinical quality measures. BMC Med. Inform. Decis. Mak. **19**(1), 44 (2019). https://doi.org/10.1186/s12911-019-0793-0

4. Chernyshev, M., Baig, Z., Bello, O., Zeadally, S.: Internet of Things (IoT): research, simulators, and testbeds. IEEE Internet Things J. **5**(3), 1637–1647 (2018). https://doi.org/10.1109/JIOT.2017.2786639

5. Di Ciccio, C., Bernardi, M.L., Cimitile, M., Maggi, F.M.: Generating event logs through the simulation of declare models. In: Barjis, J., Pergl, R., Babkin, E. (eds.) EOMAS 2015. LNBIP, vol. 231, pp. 20–36. Springer, Cham (2015). https://doi.org/10.1007/978-3-319-24626-0_2

6. Cook, D., Schmitter-Edgecombe, M.: Assessing the quality of activities in a smart environment. Methods Inf. Med. **48**, 480–5 (2009). https://doi.org/10.3414/ME0592

7. Eckleder, A., Freytag, T.: WoPeD a tool for teaching, analyzing and visualizing workflow nets. Petri Net Newsl. **75**, 3–8 (2008)

8. Elkoumy, G., et al.: Privacy and confidentiality in process mining - threats and research challenges. ACM **13**(1), 1–17 (2022). https://doi.org/10.1145/3468877. arXiv: 2106.00388

9. Gimenez, P., Molina, B., Palau, C.E., Esteve, M.: SWE simulation and testing for the IoT. In: 2013 IEEE International Conference on Systems, Man, and Cybernetics, pp. 356–361. IEEE, Manchester, October 2013. https://doi.org/10.1109/SMC.2013.67

10. Harris, C.R., Millman, K.J., Oliphant, T.E.: Array programming with NumPy. Nature **585**(7825), 357–362 (20). https://doi.org/10.1038/s41586-020-2649-2

11. Janiesch, C., et al.: The internet of things meets business process management: a manifesto. IEEE Syst. Man Cybern. Mag. **6**, 34–44 (2020). https://doi.org/10.1109/MSMC.2020.3003135

12. Jensen, K., Kristensen, L.M., Wells, L.: Coloured Petri Nets and CPN tools for modelling and validation of concurrent systems. Int. J. Softw. Tools Technol. Transfer **9**(3), 213–254 (2007)

13. Kertesz, A., Pflanzner, T., Gyimothy, T.: A mobile IoT device simulator for IoT-fog-cloud systems. J. Grid Comput. **17**(3), 529–551 (2018). https://doi.org/10.1007/s10723-018-9468-9

14. Koschmider, A., Kaczmarek, K., Krause, M., van Zelst, S.J.: Demystifying noise and outliers in event logs: review and future directions. In: Marrella, A., Weber, B. (eds.) BPM 2021. LNBIP, vol. 436, pp. 123–135. Springer, Cham (2022). https://doi.org/10.1007/978-3-030-94343-1_10

15. Papadopoulos, G.Z., Beaudaux, J., Gallais, A., Noël, T., Schreiner, G.: Adding value to WSN simulation using the IoT-LAB experimental platform. In: 2013 IEEE 9th WiMob, pp. 485–490 (Oct 2013). https://doi.org/10.1109/WiMOB.2013.6673403. ISSN: 2160-4894

16. Patki, N., Wedge, R., Veeramachaneni, K.: The synthetic data vault. In: 2016 IEEE International Conference on Data Science and Advanced Analytics (DSAA), pp. 399–410 (2016). https://doi.org/10.1109/DSAA.2016.49

17. Ramprasad, B., Fokaefs, M., Mukherjee, J., Litoiu, M.: EMU-IoT - a virtual internet of things lab. In: 2019 IEEE International Conference on Autonomic Computing (ICAC), pp. 73–83, June 2019. https://doi.org/10.1109/ICAC.2019.00019

18. Sharif, M., Sadeghi-Niaraki, A.: Ubiquitous sensor network simulation and emulation environments: a survey. J. Netw. Comput. Appl. **93**, 150–181 (2017). https://doi.org/10.1016/j.jnca.2017.05.009

19. Tremblay, J., et al.: Training deep networks with synthetic data: bridging the reality gap by domain randomization. In: 2018 IEEE/CVF CVPRW, pp. 969–977 (2018)

20. van Dongen, B.F., de Medeiros, A.K.A., Verbeek, H.M.W., Weijters, A.J.M.M., van der Aalst, W.M.P.: The ProM framework: a new era in process mining tool support. In: Ciardo, G., Darondeau, P. (eds.) ICATPN 2005. LNCS, vol. 3536, pp. 444–454. Springer, Heidelberg (2005). https://doi.org/10.1007/11494744_25

21. Wetzel, M., Koschmider, A.: Entwicklung einer VR-Umgebung zur exploration von process-mining. HMD Prax. Wirtsch. **59**(1), 37–53 (2022). https://doi.org/10.1365/s40702-021-00827-8

Author Index

Printed in the United States
by Baker & Taylor Publisher Services

Printed in the United States
by Baker & Taylor Publisher Services